ParentPreneurs

ParentPreneurs

A Decade of Deals
from a Messy Minivan

Jamie Ratner and Brian Ratner

Foreword by Kevin O'Leary

ROWMAN & LITTLEFIELD
Lanham • Boulder • New York • London

Published by Rowman & Littlefield
An imprint of The Rowman & Littlefield Publishing Group, Inc.
4501 Forbes Boulevard, Suite 200, Lanham, Maryland 20706
www.rowman.com

86-90 Paul Street, London EC2A 4NE

British Library Cataloguing in Publication Information Available

Library of Congress Cataloging-in-Publication Data

Names: Ratner, Jamie, 1977– author. | Ratner, Brian, 1974– author.
Title: Parentpreneurs : a decade of deals from a messy minivan / Jamie Ratner and Brian Ratner ; foreword by Kevin O'Leary.
Description: Lanham : Rowman & Littlefield, [2022] | Includes bibliographical references and index. | Summary: "Jamie and Brian tell their rollercoaster story of how a conversation in their minivan led to their building a multi-million-dollar company; give an honest and raw take on the toll and rewards of mixing marriage with business; and provide lessons for achieving your professional goals while balancing the demands and challenges of parenthood"— Provided by publisher.
Identifiers: LCCN 2021055987 (print) | LCCN 2021055988 (ebook) | ISBN 9781538164617 (paper) | ISBN 9781538164624 (ebook)
Subjects: LCSH: New business enterprises. | Couple-owned business enterprises. | Work and family. | Success in business.
Classification: LCC HD62.5 .R38 2022 (print) | LCC HD62.5 (ebook) | DDC 658.1/1—dc23/eng/20220121
LC record available at https://lccn.loc.gov/2021055987
LC ebook record available at https://lccn.loc.gov/2021055988

♾™ The paper used in this publication meets the minimum requirements of American National Standard for Information Sciences—Permanence of Paper for Printed Library Materials, ANSI/NISO Z39.48-1992.

For Noah and Lila
(our best deals)

Authors' Note

Throughout the book, we offer our unique and shared perspectives with a "She Said, "He Said," and "We Say" approach.

We have also tried to recreate events, locales, conversations, and experiences from our memories over a long period of time. We cannot confirm their accuracy or the accuracy of the point in time in which they took place. To protect privacy, in some instances we may have changed the names of individuals and places, and we may have changed dates or some identifying characteristics and details such as occupations, titles, and physical properties.

Contents

Foreword

My name is Kevin O'Leary. Many of you know me as "Mr. Wonderful" from the ABC television show *Shark Tank*.

I met Jamie and Brian when they appeared on *Shark Tank* in 2019 looking for an investment in their parent-focused deal website, CertifiKID. When they came into the Tank, I was blown away by how much they were asking for, but once I heard their sales numbers and strategy, I was impressed (though I don't like to show my cards). Brian fought me tooth and nail on my cut, which of course I didn't like because I'm worth it but also loved because it proved what he would be like every day, fighting for his company and my investment. Together, Jamie and Brian were an amazing team, had built a terrific and profitable company with no business background, and I was thrilled we did a deal and they joined my Shark Team family. And because I never get it wrong, they've proven this was a wise investment.

I have had the pleasure of watching them and supporting them over the past few years as they astutely navigated the challenge of scaling their business nationally in the middle of a pandemic. And they have done it by being smart, ruthless when required, and taking risks when opportunities presented themselves. Just look at their pandemic pivot acquisition of Macaroni KID, a gutsy move that catapulted their business into the largest parent-focused digital media and advertising company in the country.

There's a saying that goes, "If you want something done, give it to a busy mom." I'm a firm believer that's true, which is why I have invested in so many mom-led businesses like CertifiKID, and gotten some of my best returns from them, though I feel the same way about a "busy parent."

There are a lot of books out there, but every parent should read *ParentPreneurs*. First, it's a great read because Jamie and Brian tell a compelling story of ups and downs, successes and challenges, in both marriage and business. Second, if you're an entrepreneur like me, it will inspire you and give you important lessons on how you can build something of your own if you have a good idea, even if you don't have a formal business background or the backing from a Shark. Remember, Jamie and Brian had already built a successful company from the ground up before they came into the Tank. Lastly, the pandemic has changed forever the way we think about the value and importance of our work. Life is short and fleeting. You should do something you are passionate about and not let the traditional barriers stand in your way. You too can be a ParentPreneur like Jamie and Brian.

Now grab a glass of my wonderful O'Leary fine wine and enjoy this journey that will entertain and inspire you. And, I promise, you'll learn something.

Introduction

Jumping into the [Shark] Tank

It was 8:00 a.m. We were all piled into a white van—my husband, our children, my parents, our company's COO, and her daughter—headed for ABC Studios. Our lives had been spent preparing for this day, but we still had no idea what to expect. We were going in blind.

At seven that evening, a producer came to our trailer and told us it was time. As the golf cart neared the set, my stomach bucked. At the door to the studio, I could hear the episode filming inside—two young entrepreneurs pitched a "cooler bag." Moments later they emerged and ran down the corridor excitedly, screaming, "We got Mark Cuban!"

Well, there go our chances with him, I thought.

While we waited, I got another makeup retouch, and realized my teeth were chattering.

"Cold?" asked the lady who dusted my face with powder.

I nodded. But I wasn't cold, just shaking with fear. My daughter grabbed my hand.

"Mommy, you are going to do great," she said. I watched her get scooped up by a producer to peek at the set. And the Sharks.

We were motioned to come over, where we got to see our "set" that we had spent so much time developing. Brian was fixated on his sleeves and had been for the last two days—to roll up or not to roll up?

Who cares! I thought.

Another producer spouted off instructions, but I couldn't focus. My heart was hammering in my chest. My breath was shallow. One refrain echoed in my head:

Do not faint. Do not faint. Do. Not. Faint.

"Do you need some water, miss?" the producer asked, brow furrowed.

1

He handed me a bottle. I was suddenly surrounded by sound techs, getting "mic'd," receiving more makeup retouches, and having my hair teased.

It was the final countdown.

Brian and I had debated whether to hold hands or not when walking into the Tank. In my preparation, I had studied other entrepreneurial couples and decided that I wanted to appear strong, confident.

I don't need to hold my husband's hand! I am an independent woman!

We took a breath. The doors parted. And as we walked down the seemingly endless corridor, I reached for Brian's hand, gripped it, really. For dear life.

"There are bones in there," he whispered, smiling and squeezing back. "We got this."

I looked at him, forgetting everything.

Dear God, I thought. *What is about to happen?*

Somehow, I made it to the X on which I was supposed to stand— my "mark." We were then supposed to wait for one minute, smile and look at the Sharks but say *nothing*. The lights grew hotter by the second.

Filming began.

How the hell did we get here? I thought.

I took a deep breath and, magically, the nerves melted as I said the words that I'd recited at least a thousand times over the last few days:

"Hello. My name is Jamie Ratner, and I am the CEO & founder of CertifiKID. Today, I am here seeking $600,000 in exchange for eight percent of my business."

It was our moment. And we took it.

* * * *

When the opportunity first arose for me and my husband to audition for *Shark Tank*, I resurrected some sleuthing skills (as a former wannabe FBI agent) to try to dig up other contestants' past experiences on the show. Apparently, show producers have scared every previous contestant shitless with NDAs. If anyone ever disclosed anything, they'd get their asses sued.

But here we are—Brian and I—in this book, ready to disclose *everything* from our separate *and* shared perspectives. Well, maybe not everything, like most of the goings-on backstage when we won our investment on *Shark Tank*—we'd like to avoid legal action. But we *are* ready to disclose everything about our life in business: how we started it, how we grew it, and how we've kept our marriage and family together alongside it.

Ready?

This is the deal.

YEAR 1

How to Build Your Business on a Four-Hour Car Ride

SHE SAID: Just start Googling shit!

Every Christmas, our tradition was to go to Brian's parents' house southeast of Pittsburgh. It was December 2009, and we had our two-year-old son Noah and nine-month-old daughter Lila in the back of our packed minivan so, you know, it was *super fun.*

With nothing to distract him, I decided to tell Brian about my latest business idea. We had just signed up our son for music classes. Noah was an active kid and the music teacher wanted us to sit in a circle the whole time, but he always ran around tugging on the curtains. It was dreadful for me to keep going back week after week, but I'd already spent a fortune, so there was no way we were quitting. (I don't waste anything I pay for.)

I explained how ideal it would have been if the business had had a three-class trial pass. Without a full-session commitment, *more* families would try the class, and it would be smart for the business to get these parents in their doors at zero advertising cost.

I asked Brian the million-dollar question: what if there was a deal site that focused specifically on what *parents* want and need? "Think of the Groupon concept—but for parents," I explained.

Instead of his usual eye roll or reasons why my idea of a more family-friendly Groupon would never work (let's keep in mind I was averaging about one business idea per month), he simply said, "That's a great idea."

That simple response changed our lives.

That night, as I tried to sleep, all I could think about was this idea. I was giddy that we were actually going to do this.

Though I'd been bringing up business ideas for years, I always assumed I would have to wait until the kids were grown to start a business. Most of the moms I knew constantly complained about barely being able to take a shower, let alone go back to work or even have a second to do anything for themselves. How did I think I was going to manage this?

At that point, I truly felt like I had it all and was appreciative of my life. I had two amazing kids, a husband who provided for us (but worked more than I would have liked and was often distracted), my cushy job as a security manager at a prominent Washington, DC, law firm, my own blog, and loyal friends and family.

However, like many others, I still felt a void in my life. I could never explain it, but I just felt like I had all this creative energy that I was using in other ways: to plan amazing treehouse campouts with friends, baby showers, and even a parenting seminar group at the law firm.

It all just left me feeling flat. I wanted to build, create, and launch something of my own—something that would mean the difference between me working for someone else and me working *toward* something.

I'd never dreamed of being a June Cleaver and having cookies baked and ready for the kids when they got home. I loved having kids, but I struggled with whether being a stay-at-home mom would be enough for me. I had total mom guilt the second the kids were born about going back to my job because I wasn't that passionate about the work, and I wondered whether I was shortchanging them by putting them in daycare. I also felt concerned about missing out on social connections from not being in these "mommy groups," so I put pressure on myself to try to participate when I got home from work.

The struggle was real—and constant.

But with this new idea, I felt I might finally be able to take the plunge. I never worried when I would have *time* to do this. I never thought about what success looked like or anything like that. I never asked myself, "What happens if this doesn't work?"

My mind had a new objective: figure out what I'm doing and just go for it. The list of tasks grew and grew, and by the time I woke up the next morning, I found pages and pages sitting next to my bed ready to tackle! I know they say you're supposed to put together a business plan but, for me, I didn't plan.

I just got to work.

While the business was being born on that four-hour car ride, I quickly learned some dos and don'ts to starting a business:

1. **Pick a business name that doesn't suck.** Picking a business name is a bit like picking a long-term partner (long-term is the key here). You need to really think about the name, what it means, if it already exists, and if it makes sense as your business grows and changes. Brian immediately came up with CertifiKID but, looking back, it is one of our biggest regrets. Every single day, someone gets the name wrong, usually calling us "Certified Kid." I would highly suggest focusing on keeping your business name short, memorable, and easy to spell.

2. **Hire people who know what they're doing.** While I knew we'd need a website, I didn't have a lot of tech experience other than creating my blog. So, I hired a web developer from Craigslist. That's right, people. I said it. I posted an ad, got a good deal, and then paid for that mistake in innumerable ways. Do your due diligence, get referrals, and don't hire people off shady sites known for scams.

3. **Keep it cheap.** For a lot of people, the idea of starting a business is wildly overwhelming, especially when it comes to money. Because we were launching a digital product, we didn't have the same overhead as a physical product. Rather than come up with a budget, we used what money I had saved for my rainy-day business, which was just $5,000. From there, we decided what we would do with that money. We stuck to the budget, which was critical to our early success.

4. **Decide how many customers (or deals) you really need to launch.** Though we had little idea how we would get customers, I knew we'd need around one thousand subscribers to justify a launch. I also settled on twelve deals for the first month. By setting concrete numbers for the launch, I had a specific goal to work toward and didn't get lost in the minutiae.

What I did not know then was that there was going to be a whole "chicken before the egg" scenario for us when it came to customers and business partners. Potential business partners wanted to know we had customers before they would commit to running deals, but we needed deals to get customers to sign up. To combat this, we had to make the businesses feel like we were entering into a partnership, and as we grew, they grew. Many of these early businesses helped us out by promoting the offers to their audiences. Once I had these real moms who trusted me and my business, they were more likely to share our product with their networks. Everything spiraled out from there.

But how did we pull in the original one thousand subscribers? I engaged with real people on street corners and at parks, schools, community events, fairs, and festivals, handing out fliers, vacuuming up every email I could on my trusted legal pad. We also did a word-of-mouth and organic campaign through our personal family and friends' network via Facebook to get direct registrations.

We talked a lot on the drive about what types of businesses I would contact. Remember, we had two young children and were new to this whole parenting world. The only stuff we had really experienced so far were "Mommy and Me" classes and shopping at baby store retailers. I obviously knew there must be this whole "kids' world" out there with amusement parks and skiing trips, but we weren't thinking that big early on.

Brian immediately started worrying if there was going to be enough kid stuff for us to potentially have a new deal every day (which is comical looking back because now there are times when in the Washington, DC, market alone we have over 300 deals live). I scoured the phone book and called every class, camp, event, restaurant, birthday party entertainer and venue, play place, park, and gift shop I could think of that was geared to parents and a mom like me.

* * * *

Soon enough, launch day came.

It was Monday, May 24, 2010, at 2:00 a.m., and I was still awake and beyond exhausted but also feeling a rush of exhilaration. Our site was scheduled to launch in just a few hours. I took time off from my job in anticipation of the big day. Unfortunately, there was a glitch with our email system (said our nerdy twenty-year-old tech developer, who was still living at his mom's house).

At that point, I was totally clueless when it came to anything having to do with the technicalities of the website. Looking back, I should have read up a lot more and tried to understand what was involved.

> Remember to stay involved in your business. Here's a cringe-worthy example. A couple of months into the business, I realized I had never logged in to the domain. When I did, I looked in my spam email. Guess what was in that spam folder? An email from the producers of *The Oprah Winfrey Show* wanting to talk to me regarding an email I had sent about how the Build-A-Bear CEO's story had inspired me to finally launch this business. Freaking Oprah! When I called the producer, he told me it was too late. That was the last season of Oprah.

Despite my panic, I hit my goal of one thousand subscribers. I had invested a hundred dollars in a fake Elmo costume on eBay and was standing on the corner handing out postcards. I'd also been able to drum up a lot of buzz from my blog followers. However, I remember feeling super disappointed by a lot of friends whom I expected to be more excited and supportive about the idea but who instead seemed to look at me like I had ten heads when I explained my business. One lesson I have learned over time is that you might initially receive more surprising support and help from total strangers than from friends and family.

Outside of getting businesses signed up and nailing down subscribers, I also drummed up a lot of potential PR on my own just by emailing reporters. On launch day, a local news crew was planning to come to my house and film the launch of the site.

Our first deal was emailed out on launch morning at 6:36 a.m. for "50% off The Great Zucchini Birthday Party." Eric is a well-known local entertainer/magician who goes by the stage name "The Great Zucchini." Eric was my first "YES" and gave me the confidence that I could get businesses on board. He had quite a local following and was booked on weekends for months in advance, so we made his offer weekdays only. We promised him that he would be our first-ever deal and we would bill it as such.

Over the years, Eric ended up doing a lot of business with Certifi-KID. He seemed to appreciate how I never gave him a hard sell and always listened to him, and he came to our house to talk to us about our business and plans, while mesmerizing our kids with his tricks. We did it on a 70/30 split in his favor, which was better than the 50/50 Groupon proposal he got and what other daily deal sites were demanding.

The morning of the launch, in between dropping Noah off at his in-home daycare center and getting Lila dressed up for the launch interview, I had to jump on and off my computer and my cell phone, fielding customer service inquiries. Also, I was anxiously watching to see if any purchases were coming in.

My parents were on their way up from Baltimore to help me with the kids since we would be filming with the news crew at multiple locations. I was even able to negotiate with one of the locations—a baby store—to sponsor a CertifiKID deal.

Where was Brian during all this excitement? At work.

At last, the camera crew piled into our tiny house, set up for the shoot, got everything in place, and just as the director was about to call "Action!" Lila made a funny sound—her diaper had exploded. Perfect timing.

I excused myself and took her to her room for a change. On the way back downstairs, I couldn't help myself and refreshed the website one last time before filming. We had two sales!

I hoisted Lila into the air and cooed in her ear: "Lila, I think we might be onto something!"

Thirty days later, I quit my safe-and-secure job to focus all my energies on the business.

HE SAID: Forget perfection— it's okay if some words are misspelled!

As we started that 2009 Christmas day drive toward "the Burgh," my body was slowly tensing in anticipation of another stressful stretch through the icy mountains, with every pothole having the potential to wake Lila up. So, when Jamie unloaded the idea that would eventually lead to CertifiKID, I was singing my favorite Fleetwood Mac song and thinking, *here she goes again . . . another business idea.*

Jamie always had a new business idea and *always* talked about starting a business, which shows she is an entrepreneur at heart. I was her sounding board. It wasn't an easy job because most of the ideas I didn't understand (or think were viable, if I'm being honest), so I often found myself nodding and listening, asking questions, and encouraging her to do more research.

This was usually the pathway to the idea graveyard. For me, business was in my blood. My dad was in the car business and took over the family car dealership when his father passed away relatively young. I grew up wanting to work with my dad and take over the business from him, like he had done. I was obsessed with cars. I knew the model, make, and color of every car.

But the car industry was in terrible shape, so when my dad got an offer from the neighboring grocery store business to buy the dealership and land, he couldn't refuse. He continued working in the industry for essentially the rest of his life, but for other people.

So, without the opportunity (or pressure) to join my dad's business, I had to think about other career paths, which ultimately led me to the law, even though I always felt I had a solid business understanding from my dad's business. For example, he was the kind of car salesman who gave car salesmen a *good* name. He was loyal, honest, reliable, fair, and responsive. This created a loyal client base in an industry where that was in short supply.

But when Jamie brought up *this* idea as we were getting on Route 70 heading toward Pennsylvania from Maryland, the timing just felt off.

I was working at a start-up law firm. One year earlier, having just made partner (which was a big deal for us), the chairman of that firm—and my personal mentor—was unceremoniously removed from his position by his partners of thirty-plus years who delivered the news by simply placing a note on his chair. The next thing I knew, I was resigning from that firm to join him and start a new firm in his name. I literally walked into our house at eleven o'clock at night with a car full of boxes. Jamie was five months pregnant with our second child (Lila).

Effectively, twenty lawyers from a seventy-five-lawyer firm separated to start our own firm. (This is not a normal occurrence in the legal world and was quite a big story in the legal press.) We had no infrastructure, clients, office, or money other than the chairman's credit card—and what we each had in savings. We were working out of a friendly firm's conference room. So, at the time of this drive in late 2009, only a year into this venture, we were hanging in there, but it was not 100 percent stable.

Meanwhile, Jamie was an amazing "do it all" mom and a selfless and devoted wife. She had a great (if not unique) profession and was more than carrying her weight because she did very well financially, and the flexibility her job provided was key, allowing her to be the primary caregiver for our kids. Despite every day feeling like a fire drill, she made it all look and feel easy (even though it wasn't).

Despite our current personal and professional landscape, by the time we arrived at my parents' house, our business was born. We even discussed it with my parents, though I don't think they had a clue what we were talking about and rightly asked, "Do you really have time for this?" True, we had just been chasing our kids around the house and grabbing Noah before he went tumbling down the stairs.

But if you don't make time for your own dreams, who will?

The holiday week was supposed to be a break. I'd just completed an 80-hour work week, and the prior week I had been in London and probably had not slept more than four hours at one time in ages. But instead of relaxing, we worked into the night after the kids were asleep, threw ideas around at the local bounce place the next day, did research at halftime during the Steelers game, and made calls on the way to the local Dairy Queen. By our car ride home, *we were all in.*

When we got back, we essentially acted as if we were running a race against others, but those others didn't even know we existed (and probably still don't).

Though the timing was terrible to start a business, we believed in the idea and in each other. And maybe subconsciously, we wanted to do something together. Seriously, if you asked Jamie today what kind of law I practice, or anything about my job, I don't think she could tell you. We've been together for twenty years but, at home, we were simply going through the motions.

Despite all these doubts, uncertainties, and the bad timing, when Jamie brought up her idea at that particular moment, so enthusiastically and passionately, it got me excited too in a way I hadn't been before. In response, I did more than nod and listen.

I engaged, pushed, prodded, encouraged, and dove in equally. It surprised her. It surprised me. Like lightning in a bottle.

While Jamie was an idea machine, she also was risk-averse, so she needed me to say "YES." This was the first idea where I felt "yes" in my bones right away.

* * * *

When launch day came and the news crew rolled in, I raced to the office because I had a big filing deadline that day. (The timing, right?) It felt like the Super Bowl. Working on law stuff on one screen and watching the deal tracker on the other. Waiting one hour, then another, then another . . . and then, bam! Someone bought "The Great Zucchini Birthday Party" deal. One second later, Jamie called, and we were both freaking out like we had won the lottery.

By the end of our launch day, we had sold five vouchers, making our cut $262.50. To say that Jamie and I were both floored and ecstatic would be an understatement. Eric was quite happy and came over the next night to get his check, a practice he has continued to this day.

After the exhilaration of seeing sales come in from "The Great Zucchini" deal, reality set in, as the site kept crashing in the weeks that followed. Unsurprisingly, our Craigslist guys were rarely responsive. But when the site did work, we were selling deals, which was super encouraging. We would stay up late into the night to see our deals reach all-time highs, starting with 10, then 20, then 50, then 100, then 200, and then 1,000.

Though I understood business, I was still learning a lot. The best advice I have gotten to this day is, *If you think like a lawyer, nothing will ever get done.* To put it another way, it's okay if some words are misspelled (and with Jamie, who is an awful speller, there are a lot of misspelled words!) or if the i's and t's are not dotted and crossed perfectly. While Jamie understood this immediately, it took some adjusting for me, given my more cautious and contemplative nature. My main mindset here was, *I don't know what I don't know.* So, I needed to find and talk to the people who did.

But launching a business isn't rocket science. If you don't know something, ask people whom you trust to refer you to the person who will. Be patient in the process, do your research, talk to a lot of people, and understand that you ultimately get what you pay for. The goal isn't to do things quickly and cheaply—it's to do things in a smart and cost-effective way.

In only three months, we were profitable, more than making back the $5K we invested. We have never needed other money for CertifiKID because its profits have been able to fund the business ever since.

WE SAY: Don't let bad personal timing get in the way of a great idea.

Look, we get it. Timing matters. But when you're married with kids and have full-time jobs and endless responsibilities, the timing is *never* ideal to take a risk, right? While that may be true in theory, remember this: nothing good ever comes from just staying in your comfort zone. You want to take risks? You want to grow? You want to start a company? The only way is to just try it. Try it and fail. Try it and succeed. Keep trying until you get the results you want. While we were both nervous, we knew that starting a business while keeping our jobs was a safe bet. It allowed us to relax a little because we weren't putting our livelihoods on the line. Figure out what you're willing to risk and what you aren't—but don't ever let timing stand in the way of pursuing a dream.

YEAR 2

The First Million

SHE SAID: Don't fear or sell out because of competition.

I was in the middle of making dinner for my kids while they were melting down. They were clingy, hungry, and tired. Brian was still at the office.

Ping.

Another deal closed. Then another and another.

During CertifiKID's first eight months in business in 2010, we managed to close more than 130 deals and bring our subscriber count to 13,000. Over one thousand people purchased more than 3,000 vouchers, with our highest-volume deal selling 157 vouchers and our highest-revenue deal generating more than $8,000 in sales. In October 2011, we had hit one million in gross sales! We were stunned. Instead of celebrating or admiring our work, we did just one thing.

We went back to work.

This is probably a good time to explain again what CertifiKID is and what my pitch was to both prospective business partners and customers. Here is an example of an early email pitch I made to a local play place:

> Greetings! We are delighted to inform you of a new and can't-miss opportunity. Our business—CertifiKID—will bring scores of new, motivated, ideal, and paying customers to your door without paying a dime in advertising costs or spending personnel time to pound the pavement spreading the word about your business. If you are familiar with the websites Groupon, LivingSocial, or other group buying sites, CertifiKID is a similar concept—however, it is specifically

geared to parents, grandparents, parents-to-be, and other childcare providers in the Greater Washington area. If you are unfamiliar with the notion of group buying, it is basically a win-win proposition for the business and its customers. Each day CertifiKID will feature a single, daily, unbeatable, family value. Subscribers will be able to purchase and print their CertifiKID certificate directly on the website. Participating businesses pay nothing to be featured on CertifiKID. We make money by taking a percentage of each CertifiKID certificate we sell.

A huge challenge for businesses in this tough economic time is to get new customers in the door, especially parents constantly strapped for time. However, once you have them in the door, you are home free. In particular, mothers are very loyal customers. Research shows that 90% of moms will stay with the same brand if the product meets their expectations. Also, a huge benefit to targeting parents is that they share with each other new ideas and their favorite products and services. So the new CertifiKID customers that we bring to your door are then going to share their experience with other customers and hopefully bring in even more business.

The CertifiKID deals we hope to offer will ideally lead to savings of at least 50%. Some examples of the types of businesses we will feature are family-friendly restaurants, play gyms, family entertainment and events, family photo sessions, kid haircuts, baby-proofing services, music classes, maternity boutiques, birthday party packages, and more. From our research, we believe that your business fits perfectly into the category of business we want to promote on our website for the benefit of our subscribers—whom we believe will be the perfect customers for you. They are eager to try new and exciting local things with their families.

Reading that back a decade later, I want to cringe, but at the time, it worked! Many businesses were intrigued by the fact that there was no upfront cost. I also spent hours and hours working with each business owner and developing trust with them as I understood it was their baby and they wanted to make sure they did not cheapen their brand or fall into any of the horror stories that were being highlighted in the news with sites like Groupon overselling small businesses and crushing them.

Meanwhile, on the customer side, my goal was to get families to sign up for our email list so they would receive our deals in their inbox every day to purchase. It was free to sign up, so what did they have to lose? In the end, despite all my efforts to get customers to *just sign up*, it ended up being the deals that drove the signups. The better the deal, the more likely it was shared, and the signups came flooding in.

As we began year two, I'd never felt so energized in my entire life. Every morning, I woke up excited. I couldn't wait to see what would happen. At night, I went to bed thinking about the next day's deals.

We were doing so well that we were getting inquiries from businesses instead of making them offers. I was still handling the day-to-day customer service, sales, and marketing tasks. My dad was handling all the finances as our CFO.

Brian was still reviewing every deal before it launched and was my nightly sounding board on next steps and decisions that needed to be made, as well as my therapist and cheerleader. We were a good team. I felt that entrepreneurship was honestly what I had been missing, and that I had finally found my calling.

So, I was intrigued when I got an email from a competitor called DoodleDeals, which was interested in acquiring our business. I was also scared shitless because they were planning to expand in our area. DoodleDeals launched around the same time as CertifiKID, and their partnership with Diapers.com gave them access to an enormous customer base. One of their cofounders had exited a previous company for big money. The other cofounder and CEO was my total opposite: Ivy League, a business background, and someone who probably lunched with ladies from *Sex in the City* on the Upper East Side.

After many phone discussions, they asked if I would take a train to New York City to meet them. Of course, I said yes. I hopped an Amtrak train, leaving my kids for a full day (for the first time, I might add), and headed to Manhattan with no idea what to expect.

When I exited at Penn Station, I took the subway down to their office in SoHo, where I immediately felt intimidated. I was greeted by the CEO, who was wearing some sort of designer outfit and an overly friendly smile. I felt insecure in my cheap Banana Republic dress, which I hadn't worn since before I had kids and was years out of style.

As I was introduced to their team, I remember being amazed that they had about fifteen people who were handling all the tasks I was doing myself. My gut kept screaming that this could be an opportunity of a lifetime.

The CEO invited me to lunch. The two of us walked down a busy street in SoHo to a fancy restaurant. We chatted a bit on the walk and realized we both had children around the same age. She told me about her full-time live-in nanny and her kids' expensive private school.

When we sat down to lunch, she started to come on strong, peppering me with a lot of questions about the Washington, DC, market and going on and on about the data related to her DC email list.

Numbers can be intimidating, but I've learned they can be manipulated in any fashion to appear the most convincing. Some people are data crunchers and will make their decisions completely based on numbers. When making decisions, it's important to understand the numbers, but don't let yourself get caught up in them. Sometimes someone looks like they have a million followers on social media or says they have a million emails, but this does not mean their post about your business is going to make a bigger difference than a post by the person with ten thousand followers or emails. Ten thousand could be your sweet spot. Bigger is not always better.

We got back to the office, and I had my last meeting with their new head of sales, who had joined two weeks earlier. He wasn't a parent. I was instantly concerned that he couldn't possibly know what a mom wants and needs, which was the entire essence of our business. He started telling me how I would be on "his" sales team. This was the first time I had ever been referred to as a salesperson.

When I got home late that night, Brian was on the couch watching *The Real Housewives of New York City* (his guilty pleasure) while tapping away on his laptop, looking totally drained from the workday plus taking on my evening routine. I crashed on the couch next to him and pulled out the black and white cookies I had picked up at the train station, which we started devouring.

"I don't know what to do," I said. "Do we go with this giant and possibly reap the rewards of their experience, size, connections, and expertise, or stay the course and possibly get crushed and taken out for good?"

I told him I couldn't imagine having a boss or being a salesperson. That's why I left my job and started this business in the first place. I was used to having Lila home with me a couple of days during the week and making my own schedule, and I was worried they were going to tell me I needed to work full time in an office.

After much hand-wringing that night, and the next few nights, we decided to pass on the deal. I said it came down to the fact that I didn't want to be someone's employee. They were gracious and said they understood.

> When I met with one of their young sales reps during my meeting at the DoodleDeals office, she was tasked with calling on some of my reference vendors. I gave her three names. One was a jewelry maker whom I had become very close with. I'd spent hours cultivating that relationship. A few days after I declined their offer, I had an email from the vendor:
>
>> Just spoke with someone from DoodleDeals. She was really nice and gave me a chance to talk about how awesome you are! Speaking with her made me realize that I don't really understand what it is that you do—she is blown away that you do it all yourself. :) She went to my website and is now interested in running me on her site, which has 120K on the mailing list (holy cow!).
>
> What. The. Actual. Fuck.
>
> Instantly, I realized they had poached the vendors I supplied as references! It became crystal clear that there are no rules in business, and I no longer felt any regret about my decision.

* * * *

Meanwhile, I carried on with mixed feelings of fear and relief, but I dove into the creative side of the business, which only I could do as my own boss. I spent so much time brainstorming and getting uber-creative with these business owners on ways to market their businesses and draw traffic to help them grow. These innovative deals were not always making lots of money but were truly giving our business a unique flavor and creating special relationships and partnerships that differentiated us from the Groupon clones out there.

For example, we finally landed an account with Whole Foods. It started when I noticed a purchase on our site made by a person with an email ending in wholefoods.com. (I'm sure you're wondering why I was looking at the emails of each individual purchaser. It's a good question. At that time, I was looking at EVERY purchase that was made EVERY day. I was paying attention to all things—big and small—with the business.)

I decided to write immediately to her, asking if she might have the contact information for the Whole Foods marketing director. She replied right away, and after a quick exchange, it became clear that *she* was the marketing director for a nearby location, which happened to be a one-minute drive from my house, and was available to meet with me right away.

I quickly changed out of my yoga pants, put on something present-able, told Brian he needed to watch the kids and get dinner ready, and I literally jumped in my car and headed to the store, not wanting to blow this insane chance. During our meeting, my new contact was will-ing to give us only a fruit cake deal. What? Seriously. We moaned and groaned, worried that people would think it was a joke. But we figured we could start with this single offer and then build our relationship from there. And to our amazement, the deal sold out! We were ecstatic. This led to many other offers with Whole Foods and a great relationship, which shows that sometimes you must be willing to start somewhere.

On the other side of the food chain, I was approached by a company called Rent a Chicken Coop that wanted to run a deal. This is a business where you rent chickens to teach your kids about the ecosystem, and they lay eggs, which you can eat. We had no idea how it would perform and were concerned people would think it was too far out there, which could diminish our credibility. But when the email for the deal went out, our open rates went through the roof, as everyone just wanted to learn more, and then the deal sold exception-ally well. We have run it multiple times since then. Overall, these somewhat quirky deals reinforced that it was worth taking risks and giving new ideas a chance.

If we had sold out to DoodleDeals just because we were worried about competing with them, I would have missed these other great opportunities.

HE SAID: Some of the best deals are the ones you *DON'T* do.

In year two, I fought the commute home (and road rage) from my day job at the firm and slowly eased my way through the front door. Noah jumped on my back, and I winced with a crooked smile. I then walked to the fridge where Lila stood in front of it pointing and yelling, POPSICLE!"—with the look of a bank robber standing in front of a teller.

I opened the freezer and heard Jamie scream at me to not give her another one because she'd already had two. I started to close the freezer and the bank robber started freaking out, so I snuck her one and told her to go hide in a corner. Jamie yelled from the other room, "I know you just gave her one!"

Strike one.

I then ate my frozen meal because Jamie, who is an amazing cook, was a bit too distracted to make the gourmet meals I had gotten accustomed to from our pre-kids (and pre-CertifiKID) days. And then I met Jamie on the couch so she could walk me through my nightly homework: edit five deals, review three contracts, and discuss for the fiftieth time whether we should get bought out by DoodleDeals or not. She snapped at me when I got distracted by the TV, as if I'd been on vacation all day and needed no downtime of my own.

Strike two.

By the time midnight rolled around, I had passed out with Jamie still typing away on her laptop and Lila sleeping between us, attached to Jamie's leg.

Strike three.

In terms of the business, I was the last pair of eyes on every deal we ran, doing the final edits and proofing. At this point, we were running a deal a day and it was a *lot* of work to edit at ten o'clock every night. Jamie was always a step ahead of me, so it was super frustrating for her to be waiting for me every day to do the last 10 percent. And then, of course, there was constant pressure knowing that she could do more if I was able to keep up with her.

Yes, we were making money and not spending much of it. Jamie's dad, Gary, was doing the books, which was a huge help to both of us because of how much trust we had in him. He treated every cent like it was his own and worked harder than before he had retired from his old job. But Jamie felt the heat of our competitors.

When LivingSocial started a family edition directly competing with CertifiKID in our home Washington, DC, market, it took everything to another level. In one sense, it was validating that a company valued at $500+ million would buy in to the local niche we started. But how could Jamie and our small team compete with an army of iPad-carrying, Ivy League–educated salespeople?

Every night, Jamie would lie in bed, sleep-deprived when Lila insisted on sleeping with us, and say the business was going to die the next day. (And she'd throw in that no one could pronounce "CertifiKID" and would keep calling it "Certified KID." Humph.) She made me promise to her that it didn't matter if it *did* die, and that we had to handle all our finances with this mindset. She didn't want the pressure. When she wasn't scared about the business dying, she was desperate to quit before it did. So, I'd have to talk her off the ledge again and again and again.

I'd explain the numbers, show her the numbers, and pull up the bank account. But she didn't care or believe it. It was an alternate reality.

Passing on DoodleDeals and building our own core team helped pave the way to our first million. Many people want to know how we got there and so quickly.

The CertifiKID secret sauce was created from a mixture of these ingredients (*hint: lean and mean with low expenses and a focus on profitability as much as growth*), which are reflected throughout this book and can translate as lessons for any other start-up:

1. **Keep expenses low—at all costs!** Sounds easy, right? Wrong! Some businesses struggle with this. We had the mindset to generally keep our out-of-pocket expenses low, especially in the first two years, and still do. The question Jamie would always ask is, "Do we really need this?" Ask yourself the same. For example,

   • We maintained a home office and virtual workplace, so no overhead.
   • We had a lean staff, with only necessary personnel on a W-2 basis, and all sales personnel working on a success-based

independent contractor model. This enabled us to recruit excellent team members attracted to the flexibility of the job.
- Our investments in our website and technology were proportionate to what we were making, so we only invested more in these AFTER we saw the business growing at an early stage. While crucial to any internet-based business, we think it is a strategic error to spend time and money on technology or any one aspect of the business BEFORE you have shown proof of concept.
- Jamie did not take a salary or any money out of the business other than to pay taxes in the first two years, even though we had generated $1 million in sales. She only started taking a salary in 2013 when our accountants recommended it because they were concerned that our revenue and profitability levels would provoke an IRS audit. Meanwhile, my work as president and Gary's work as CFO were uncompensated, which saved the business a fortune over ten years. Thus, the management team for the business was uncompensated in the first two years, thereby not dragging down profitability.
- Our external lawyer was one of my best friends growing up, and our accountants were with the same firm I used with my law firm, so we trusted them and could ensure their costs were proportionate. For example, my buddy didn't send us a bill for the first three years. One could say this was just lucky or that we were connected, but the point is to get help from people you trust and only pay for it when you absolutely need to or have no other options.

2. **Focus on organic growth first.** We grew organically, mainly through word of mouth, social media, partnerships, and bartering without substantial investments in marketing or customer acquisition. It's vital to prove the concept first, using real people—not "bought" interest.
3. **Assume limited debt.** We sought to limit our debt, so that when we became profitable in the third month, we simply reinvested profits into the business, avoiding the need to seek external financing or investment from family, friends, or venture capital ("VC") sources.

4. **Prove your concept and build your pipeline.** During the second year, we were making good money each month. We ran a deal a day. We were building our pipeline. And then, BOOM! We had two homerun deals, an Urban Pirate Cruise in the Baltimore Harbor and Chesapeake Beach Water Park, which together sold more than 3,500 vouchers. This was the biggest exclamation point on our proof of concept and fueled Jamie to push harder. The success of these deals then compounded because we could use them as templates for what any new business could achieve on our platform. These were not mom-and-pop shop results, and no business or competitor could legitimately suggest otherwise.

5. **Go deep and local before scaling.** We went "deep and local" in our home Washington, DC/Baltimore market and chose not to follow the herd by expanding beyond this region with local or national deals in the first two years, unlike other competitors.

6. **Great customer service saves you money and makes you money.** We had unmatched customer and member service. Jamie would answer customer calls at 11:00 p.m. on a Saturday and they were shocked the *CEO* was on the other end of the phone. We would issue refunds like candy and suck up the losses on transaction fees. This approach created loyalty with our subscribers, so they made multiple purchases and spread the word.

7. **Stay lean and mean.** We didn't work from a three- or five-year business plan. Our plan was day to day—we (with Jamie as the leader of our flock) simply watched the space like a hawk, followed the positive trends, and avoided the negative ones. Looking back, sometimes we were too late to a trend and would often kick ourselves over how much more we could have done in the first two years if we were a bit quicker at key stages. But we were lean and mean and couldn't do it all, so we had to accept this reality and its limitations. The bottom line was that this approach helped us vastly more than it hurt us over time.

8. **Embrace and exploit your differentiators.** We learned from other competitors how different our business model was. They

had VC financing. We didn't. They had expensive office space. We didn't. They had spent a fortune on technology before launching. We hadn't. They had a big C-suite and sales staff, including many on substantial salaries. We didn't.

Yes, we lost something by not spending more money earlier and making more investments in marketing and customer acquisition. But had we done so, we likely would have struggled just like everyone else, and then needed to bring in external financing to keep growing and stay afloat.

9. **Maintain control as long as you can.** By passing on opportunities like DoodleDeals and maintaining control over our business, we had no one else to answer to or report to, which allowed us to be nimble and flexible and take risks on new deals and partnerships. For example, we imposed an unwritten policy that we would NEVER lose out on a deal that we wanted—big or small—because of pricing. So, we would undercut Groupon, LivingSocial, and anyone else with our percentage (e.g., Groupon wanted 50 percent of every sale, and we would do 40 percent, 30 percent, 25 percent or whatever it took to make a deal happen), which encouraged so many businesses to give us a try.

   We could do this only because we had *control*. Other businesses had to operate with a one-size-fits-all mentality at that stage because of their overhead and cost infrastructures. Ironically, several years later, with few competitors standing, there was a huge race to the bottom with pricing in the market because Groupon and everyone else was desperate to get any revenue they could to meet their quarterly targets and expectations. We never had to worry about these pressures and could simply focus on win-win arrangements with our merchant partners. This shows that some of the best deals are the ones you DON'T take.

10. **Knowing your worth will prevent you from making bad deals.** Our unique model ultimately led to our #1 ingredient—that we were a true resource for families and not just a deal site. This came through in the quality and variety of our offerings and unmatched customer service. But we realized our true worth and potential only because of the deals we *didn't* do.

**WE SAY: Think of the glass half full when you start,
and then half empty when you succeed.**

With our success (and the opportunities that came with it), it was easy for Brian to see the glass half full. But Jamie also saw the glass half empty as we considered expansion, fought the competition every day, and still struggled to grow our subscriber base and our team. By staying hungry and never resting on our laurels when we hit those seven zeros, *we* were able to focus on the task ahead: growth.

YEAR 3

Surviving Marriage, Parenthood, and Business

SHE SAID: Money brought some relief from fear, but no pleasure.

"It's moving day!"

I yelled to the kids and wiped away the sweat. It was June and would be one of the hottest days DC would see that summer. I eagerly checked our deal stats because we had sent out an email that morning for the "Hottest Deals of the Summer to Deal with the Summer Heat."

I got the kids dressed and fed. The movers had just arrived to start filling up their truck for the trek to our new home, which was only five miles (but felt like a world) away from our current home. I prayed Brian would make it through the day because, on our last moving day, he had ended up in the hospital with a debilitating headache caused by food poisoning from a smoothie he drank in a market in Thailand.

Now that we were profitable, we decided it was time to move from our adorable but small single-family home to a house that had space for our kids to run around, a proper office for me (because I had been working in our breakfast nook), and a bigger bedroom for Lila than the giant closet she was currently inhabiting. We loved being close to the city, but it was time to head to the suburbs. The most exciting part of the move was the pool.

> I do not recommend buying a house with a pool. As dreamy as it seems, it is a giant money pit that forces you to constantly entertain, and you will always be afraid a kid will drown or get hurt on your watch.

We all loaded up in our packed minivan and headed down the road to the new house. The kids were super excited, and Lila was looking forward to seeing her freshly painted pink and purple room. Noah was more focused on the pool and yard.

I was just thrilled it had a big basement for the kids to run around in so I could finally get some work done. I *had* learned a bunch of tricks over the years for managing the kids while working at the same time. My best move was the hide-and-seek trick. Whenever I knew I had a super important call, I would make sure I was the "seeker," and it would somehow take me until the end of the call to find them!

When we got to the house, it was filled with contractors who were trying to complete painting and final touches on the floors before the movers got there. Just then, I realized how chaotic the next couple of weeks were going to be. There was still work we needed to do, but at least the bedroom floor was finished so we could sleep well.

After getting everything moved in, we were exhausted. In the middle of the night, we heard heavy rain outside and then were shaken by a huge crashing sound. Noah came racing into our room. Lila was already huddled between us because we could not get her out of the habit of coming into our bed. All the power had gone out. We quickly realized this was not a typical storm and swiftly headed down to the basement to be safe, navigating our way around endless stacks of boxes.

In the morning, we awoke to a bleak situation. The power was still out. The temperature was supposed to be hotter than the day before. And then we looked in horror at the backyard to see that a gigantic tree had fallen onto our pool cover and broken through it, while several other trees had also been struck down.

As Brian worried about the pool and trees, I was freaking out because we had no power, no AC, and no Wi-Fi. I needed to make sure everything was okay with the day's email blast and that things were running smoothly.

We then began to realize this "derecho" storm was even bigger than we thought. The whole city was without power, and trees were down all over the area. Everything was closed. Luckily it was a Saturday, so the city had two days to recover. However, when you own a Web-based business, it's open 24/7, and I needed to get Wi-Fi to keep everything running smoothly.

We heard that the mall had power, so we headed there, and I set up my laptop on the floor near an electrical socket while Brian watched the kids run around a little play area next to a hundred other desperate parents. While subconsciously weighing the odds of the kids catching some illness in that overcrowded play area, I tried to focus on making sure these emails were ready to send. (Priorities!)

The next few days, our house was again filled with contractors working on the renovations—painting and new carpet. Brian's family reunion of forty-plus people was taking place in a week—and I had been tasked with planning it. Not to mention I needed to unpack our sea of boxes.

To say I was feeling the stress and pressure would be a massive understatement.

I won't bore you with the details but, by the time Brian walked through the door at the end of his workday, he was enemy number one. It didn't matter that he too was working his ass off and had a mountain of stress on his shoulders. All I could think about was how much I had weighing on *my* shoulders, and I didn't know how to ease the pressure.

Years later, I still don't. I wish I could offer some genius advice for couples to brew up an extra couple of hours in their day just for each other, but stress always seems at an all-time high and time is a hot commodity.

It really does come down to your mindset: realizing your spouse isn't an enemy and that stressful situations are isolated moments. They are temporary. Relationships are long term. Reminding yourself of this when shit gets hard is critical.

Because shit *always* gets hard, regardless of circumstance.

* * * *

I was twenty-three years old when I met Brian and had just graduated from grad school the day before. I had moved back home from Boston to Maryland and was having a reunion night with three of my closest friends. We went to a bar and my friend Laurie ran into her brother's friends, which included Brian who had also recently moved to town from LA. Not only did I think he was one of best-looking guys I had ever met, he was very sweet and easy to talk to. My friends and I left the bar that night and I told my single friends they should totally go for that guy and were crazy if they didn't . . . because I was in a long-term relationship at the time. A few days later, Laurie told me that Brian had inquired about me to her brother Dave, which I stored away in my subconscious. Months later when my relationship ended (on 9/11!), I mentioned to my friend to pass along word to her brother, who would hopefully pass along word to Brian. The next thing I knew, Brian called, and we went out on our first date. I knew I wanted to marry him right away (though after our third date, where we spent an hour looking for a parking space as opposed to simply following a person to their spot like I still tell him to do to this day, I was seriously minutes away from throwing in the towel). I remember calling him Brandon Walsh (from *Beverly Hills, 90210*) to my friends because I could not believe how perfect he was. He checked all the boxes, and I was head over heels!

Over time, once the honeymoon phase passed, I realized he isn't perfect (which is a normal awakening in all relationships). He drives me nuts with his need for cleanliness (I'm a slob), having to say goodbye to every person when leaving a party (I always want to sneak out early), correcting my grammar and misspellings (not my strong suit), and being what I called Mr. Money Bags (I'm frugal). However, what *is* perfect is how the two of us complement each other in many ways. We are very different people, but it works. I love my time with him no matter what we are doing—from the crappy stuff to the fun stuff.

The thing is, prior to having kids and running a business together, I feel like Brian and I had time together to really reflect on and work through issues in our relationship. From dinners to cooking classes to getaways in the mountains, we spent time cultivating our relationship. And now?

Now it was all about survival.

This journey through marriage, business, and parenthood has been full of learning. The biggest lessons I have learned to date are these:

1. **The best way to raise happy, well-adjusted children is to maintain a safe, strong, and happy marriage. Happy kids do not make a good marriage. So, it is important you make your marriage a top priority.** Kids can *feel* when things are not right and that can make them anxious or act out. I grew up in a home where my parents never fought or raised their voices. Brian grew up in a very loud house. We tend to work somewhere in

the middle. Our kids see us constantly bickering about the business (and the writing of this book!), and I am sure they have become accustomed to understanding that arguments are just part of life. If either of us steps over the line with each other in not being respectful, it is obvious by my daughter's anxious demeanor. It's important for me that we acknowledge her anxiety so she understands we are working through a business issue and will eventually land on the same page (which we always do once we hash things out).

2. **If something is bothering you, don't hold it in.** Whether it is the business, co-parenting, or our sex life (or nonexistent sex life when our daughter is in our bed every night!), it is important to speak up and not expect your spouse to be a mind reader. I have found it cathartic to journal when I have time. I have many friends who see therapists regularly and find them to be amazing, but journaling is super easy (and free!). By the time I'm done, I usually realize I have figured out what's at the root of how I'm feeling. I'm able to look at it from a new perspective.

3. **Marriage and parenting are not always going to be 50/50.** Some days it feels like me 80/Brian 20, and then one weekend it will feel like Brian 75/me 25. Just don't keep score. Do the best you can do—with and for each other. I think we both have always tried to make life easy for the other person. I get frustrated because I am a planner and feel like if Brian could *just* think in advance, there could be more we could accomplish. But on the flip side, when he surprises the kids and comes home early to take them on an outing, I have a spontaneous two hours to myself. Instead of looking at your partner's differences as flaws, look at the positives those attributes create.

4. **Remember how lucky you are.** Most importantly, whether we are in a business meeting or at a parent-teacher conference, I am always trying to take a moment to step back and remind myself how lucky I am to have this incredible person by my side whose strengths are my weaknesses, who always has my best interests at heart, and who truly is my best friend. I am awful at vocalizing my appreciation and would certainly say I am anything but lovey-dovey. However, I think being aware of

what you have is important. Remember to constantly check in with yourself because your feelings often come out in your actions. Make sure those actions come from a place of kindness and gratitude, even when the house is dirty, the kids aren't fed, and you just want to scream. You're lucky.

HE SAID: Sharing a purpose outside of your kids is a healthy distraction from the pressure of parenthood.

For this chapter, I was instructed to get real about our marriage and how we survived parenthood in this year and those that followed. To show how bad I am at this, I had to rewrite the chapter five times. I wasn't *emoting* enough and wasn't "getting it," Jamie said.

As hard as this may be to believe, it wasn't until we started writing this book that Jamie told me she had been writing in her journal ever since I met her. She would do it in her alone time.

"What alone time?" I immediately asked. *She had alone time? When? How? I wanted some!*

I never saw her write. (And I'm sure I'd be horrified to read it!) But this admission made me sad—both that I didn't know and worse that I hadn't noticed. It also made me happy that she had an outlet and a way of surviving that could help center her in a way I obviously couldn't.

* * * *

Meanwhile, at the beginning of our relationship and before kids, we felt like we had it all.

The irony of Jamie and I meeting in a bar is that neither of us are drinkers. We'd have a drink socially but were both tame. After the night we met, I honestly can't remember the two of us ever going to a bar together, or meeting others at a bar. We may have but I can't recall a time. I remember having an easy conversation that night with her. While I am three years older than she is, we both went to Big Ten schools and our friends ran in some of the same circles (or were siblings!), so we had a good bit in common and to talk about. I remember thinking how cute she was and loving her smile and laugh. Also, I had just moved to the area earlier in the year but it was her hometown, so I remember her telling me she was a foodie and giving me some restaurant recommendations.

I was excited when I learned from my friend that she was now single. I called her and we had a great first date at a sushi restaurant (which to this day is our family's favorite dinner spot) near her apartment in Bethesda, Maryland, which was about fifteen minutes from my place in Georgetown. She always jokes that she was immediately hooked on me because I overordered and agreed to share our sushi that night, which we do to this day. For Jamie, it's never about eating one meal, it's about trying as many items as possible.

Our fourth date was a highlight as she got courtside tickets to see the Wizards who had Michael Jordan playing for them that season. I'm a sports buff, given my Pittsburgh roots, so I was thrilled to see him play in person for the first time, let alone in such amazing seats. Jamie does not like watching sports in person or on TV, so I think it was the first and last time she went to any sports event other than a Harlem Globetrotters game with our kids because we got free tickets through CertifiKID.

After we were dating for a while, I took her home to meet my parents for a family wedding, which certainly made them think it was serious. She got along well with my folks and sister right from the start. The fact she is quiet and easygoing with a great sense of humor made her a perfect fit for my lively, warm, and outgoing family.

Her lovely parents are the same way so when they met mine over brunch at a Pancake House (which to this day is our family's favorite brunch spot), they too hit it off. Like Jamie and me, our families complemented each other as well. For example, Jamie and her family are always early and proactive about making plans, reservations, saving tables, and so on, while my family and I are always on time or a bit late and can procrastinate.

After a year, we knew we were in love and it was meant to be, so we moved into a condo together in DC, which was really "easy living" with the amenities of a doorman, pool, and parking. We then bought a row house a year after that outside Georgetown. The house was ideal as we rented out the basement to a Georgetown University med student which helped pay the mortgage. On the other hand, the neighbors were a group home for persons with intellectual disabilities, and we were awakened in the middle of most nights by banging on our walls. We got married while living in that house but, as soon as we could sell and make a big profit, we jumped at the chance and bought our first single-family home in Bethesda.

During this time from dating until kids, we had a vibrant social life and spent time together when I wasn't working. We'd go to the gym, take runs, or just explore the city. While I was burning the midnight oil and advancing at my law firm, Jamie moved jobs a few times, but all the positions were positive steppingstones in the security profession and came with a good work-life balance. Her schedule also allowed her to make us amazing gourmet dinners every night; plan exotic trips for us to places like Thailand; organize fun activities and trips for ourselves and with our family and friends; and join me on international business trips. Life was good.

It got even better when we started our family. Noah was born in 2007, and Lila followed nineteen months later. We were beyond thrilled to have a boy and a girl but two kids under two is a tall order and we were just getting by.

While we did it willingly, the business was an earthquake to our marriage and family. How could it not be?

* * * *

The hard truth is that working together and running a business with your spouse (even a successful multimillion-dollar one) is VERY HARD (AND STRESSFUL). It takes a toll. And you give up a great deal. We could have grown our family (Jamie used to talk about four kids!) but chose not to. We could have had date nights, but we gave them up. We could have basked in alone time. (I still have zero clue what this is.) We could have been romantic and intimate more often. (I'm sure Jamie keeps tabs on this.) We could have had more focused time with our kids. Time to chill. Time to rest. Time to recover. Time with our friends. Time to embrace the culture and important issues around us.

For example, 2012 was the year Barack Obama was reelected president. I'm a politico, and an active one at that. I care about the world in which we live and have opinions about our future. And it was a big deal for me. Jamie is not active or involved politically at all and often wondered whether my focus on this was a waste of time.

And while Jamie has somehow also been the primary caregiver to our kids, I do think these losses and this tension within our marriage have hit me equally hard because I have been balancing another job and commitment that I also care passionately about, and that is very important for our family. Therefore, the guilt of not having enough time for that work has caused stress and insecurity as well. I am a people pleaser, so I want to make everyone happy. Jamie thinks this is BS and that much of what I do, I don't actually *have* to do—that it's my choice and by trying to do it all, I'm in la-la land and not doing anything well.

Unfortunately, it's often just all half-assed because with the time I give myself for things, that is all it can be. It's my choice and personal struggle, and I know I'm always sacrificing something.

Would I have wanted Jamie to stay part-time in her prior job which had a work-life balance and was more than we needed from a financial standpoint, or be a partner who was more lovey-dovey and more of a housewife who took care of everything (including me) with a smile on her face, spent her days exercising, lunching with friends, and running the PTA?

Maybe subconsciously, I yearn for this when times are difficult, I am frustrated, and I know she is frustrated with me. It would be easier for sure and would require me to sacrifice less.

But mainly, I am so proud of my wife and would not want her to be doing anything else other than what she is doing now because she is good at it and an inspiration. We have built a great business, and it fills her up in many ways. She has supported me and helped me succeed, so if I held her back, it would be selfish. I'm not saying this because it sounds good or because I am some "super feminist." I'm saying it because her success fills me with pride and shows our kids (and especially our daughter) that their mom's work is as important to our family as mine is.

When it's "Go to Work with Parents" day, the kids want to stay home with Mom. I love this. At the end of the year, they ask, "Who won?" Like who had a better year, Mom or Dad? Sometimes Dad and sometimes Mom. I love this too. We have made each other more successful and more professionally fulfilled, even if that means we have sometimes sacrificed our own personal fulfillment to get there.

Should I have cut the cord on either the business or the firm? (In other words, pick one instead of trying to do both.) Jamie always says she would love it if I would join the business full-time and work from home with her.

Though I wonder if she'd want to kill me, she doesn't think she'd have the same reaction to me being in her space versus the assistants she couldn't handle. I think I could do it, and there would be a lot I would enjoy. It would bring my stress level down. I'd eat better, and exercise more. My travel time would go way down. I'd be there when the kids got up in the morning and returned from school. I'd help with homework and carpools. I'd be able to be more active in the community.

But I'd also give up the legal profession I worked hard to build. And I'd give up on a firm that I helped create from scratch and feel a sense of ownership over. It didn't come easily. I'm an overachiever. So many people I work with are smarter than I am, with far more brilliant legal minds. While I have risen in the ranks of my firm, they wouldn't miss me. But I'd give up the financial upside and security that allows us to take risks with the business we wouldn't otherwise. My job gives Jamie the comfort that the business could fold tomorrow, and we would be okay.

I think deep down Jamie likes the setup. I don't believe my being home will help us with the business in any way drastically different from now. I know Jamie understands that I enjoy my legal profession and feel too committed to my firm and its future to give it up, even if she doesn't always understand the choices I make about my schedule.

The issue is that we know these are our respective choices and understand they reflect who we are as individuals. But then I wonder why we don't give each other a break, let it go, and support each other. Seriously, we still don't!

Years later, I moan about not giving enough support to Jamie and the business. I don't credit or acknowledge what she does for me and the kids every day. I groan about the house being messy (though the groaning is inaudible at this point), and instead of saying anything, I just come home and start picking up after her and the kids.

Meanwhile, there are still no hugs or kisses when I get home from a trip like there used to be, no questions about how my day was, and no sympathy when she knows I have been stressed at work or doing something difficult. Jamie and I joke when I get sick that she is a great caregiver—making me soup, meals, waiting on me hand and foot—but there is NO sympathy, no warm clothes, cuddling, or comforting. It's probably because when she is sick, she works through it and I'm not there to take care of her. While she thinks I treat her like a secretary, she forgets I'm her personal banker (yes, she is the CEO of a multimillion-dollar business but still doesn't know how to take money out of an ATM!), lawyer, financial advisor, accountant, and weekend chauffeur.

Frick and frack.

But despite our different personalities and often divergent approaches to our life, marriage, and work, we carried on and found a way to lean on each other. Sometimes we would fight (usually about me not listening and her being a slob, or any of the above peculiarities). Sometimes we would be strangers passing in the night (her up to bed as soon as I came home late and me going to work before the sun came up while she was still sleeping). But most of the time, we were deeply engaged with each other regarding the business and the kids. And because I often felt the guilt of not being there enough with the kids and Jamie carrying much of the weight, whereas Jamie felt resentment for the same reasons, the business was an outlet and a healthy distraction.

We were talking about building something, using our minds with less emotion, and supporting each other with our different skills and roles. And we trusted each other, so despite our frustrations, we knew we both had the same motives and goals—to help each other and the business and not just make a lot of money (though that was a nice byproduct). Yes, the romance and intimacy would often take a backseat in this period as we dealt with the highs and lows of the business, but the shared purpose, commitment, and effort brought us closer together in other ways.

And we would soon have time to catch up on what we had sacrificed—but never fully, and always feeling like it was a work in progress, which we still do feel to this day. Because the business would always pull us back in. It was and is a huge commitment that has only gotten bigger over time with immense responsibility and pressure. But it works because it's shared sacrifice and a labor of love.

To summarize some words of wisdom, which we are still trying to follow ourselves as we go through our daily game of survivor,

1. **Give each other a break.** Don't just accept your different choices and sacrifices. Embrace and support them.
2. **Find a *shared* experience outside the kids.** Whether it's a business, hobby, recreation, cause, or issue, find something else that can be a healthy distraction from the day-to-day monotony of life and parenthood.

3. **Find your own *personal* outlet and support your spouse's.**
They don't have to be the same thing! Whether it's a journal,
therapy, exercise, politics, or a sport, get that personal fulfillment, which will help create a healthy mind, body, and spirit.
And actively support your spouse's right to self-care!

4. **Don't waste time being passive-aggressive—be aggressive.**
You can't read each other's minds. Let it out and move on.

5. **The kids can't always be the excuse.** The kids are an easy
distraction, but they can't always be the main excuse for not
communicating.

6. **Trust your foundation.** If you have the foundation of love and
trust, you can overcome anything. Don't give up on each other.
What you can't do now, or don't have time for now, doesn't
mean you won't tomorrow.

WE SAY: Time together will come, and it's worth the wait.

When our kids got older and we were able to send them to overnight
summer camp for seven weeks (trust us, they wanted to go), we were
granted the gift of extensive kid-free time for the first time in years.
That first summer, we felt the same feeling parents probably have when
they drop their kids off at college—this insane rush of freedom! Life
shifted, and with the kids not the primary focus, we were able to focus
on our relationship and have fun together.

We went for runs on the beach and walks around the neighborhood. We went to dinner and wouldn't talk only about the business. We
visited with family and friends we hadn't seen in a while. We traveled to
places near and far. We caught up on our latest Netflix binge-watching
and went to the movies. We slept in. We practiced yoga together. All
the worry subsided about what the relationship was lacking during
those hard years.

We know few have the luxury (or the desire) to send their kids
off to camp, let alone for almost two months. But if you have a strong
foundation, when the time comes for you to get any extended period
of uninterrupted time together, you won't regret those past missed date
nights or the mom nights out on the town. You will cherish every drop
of time you *do* have together as a couple and as a family.

· 4 ·

YEAR 4

Growing Pains

SHE SAID: If you're in charge, act like it.

LESLIE: You there?

ME: Yep.

LESLIE: I am putting up a deal for the Bread Store.

ME: Ok. What is it?

LESLIE: It is a $12 for $15, "weekday only" deal.

ME: Leslie . . . you know that won't sell.

LESLIE: I know, but I feel bad for him. He needs the business.

ME: I don't think you should do it.

LESLIE: Too late. I already made it live on the site.

This exchange was my world. I was supposed to be the boss but was just not there yet in getting people to treat me like one. I had never been a boss really (unless you consider the one summer when I was a camp counselor in charge of my bunkbed, which wasn't an experience that gave me a lot of confidence), so I had no idea how to act like one and get the respect I deserved.

Because of how well the business was doing (at least that's what Brian and my dad kept telling me), I knew we needed to focus on building a strong team, and I had to start delegating. I wouldn't let Brian get us an office, as I wanted to continue to operate leanly and freely at home, so we had the extra challenge of building and running a team virtually.

We had several team members at this point who were mainly working on an independent contractor basis, though we knew we needed to make some key positions more permanent to take advantage of our opportunities. This was a tough decision for me. I was terrified of having other people's livelihoods dependent on the success of *my* business. As a fatalist, it was hard enough thinking that my own livelihood would somehow change if the business ended tomorrow.

My Core Team (to this day): Every business needs one.

I'll start with Leslie. About six months after the launch of the business, I sent an email to the CertifiKID audience announcing that we were expanding from our Washington, DC, home market into Baltimore and were looking to hire. That afternoon, my phone rang. When I answered, the woman on the other end of the line (with a very engaging voice) just started talking. Her name was Leslie. She explained to me that she saw our job posting and initially thought of her friend for it, but the more she contemplated it through the course of the day, the more she realized SHE would be a good fit for this job. She proceeded to ask me a thousand questions, and I naively and patiently answered all of them. The call ended with her telling me she would get started that night and she had some ideas. *What in the world just happened? Had this lady just hired herself?* The answer was "yes."

Leslie jumped in with full force and never once asked about money or signed any sort of employment contract. It was only later that Brian made me put something official in writing with her. She had a "real" job, which she kept for several years before finally cutting the cord and joining CertifiKID full time. After she started, we finally met in person, and it was clear she was quite the character. She was about seven years older than I was, a bit disheveled, and wore no makeup. She spoke to every person who crossed her path. But the more we talked, the more I realized how much we had in common.

Over time, Leslie not only became the secret weapon of our business but one of my best friends (another surprise of starting a business— the gift of making personal connections and relationships you would not have otherwise). I have learned from her and am grateful for all she has taught me and everything she puts into the business. I'm amazed she has stuck with us for this long, though I know she would say she is amazed we have put up with her for this long!

Here are some lessons I learned from Leslie and why she is the best salesperson I have ever met:

1. **Take risks.** Right off the bat, I realized this girl doesn't like rules or to color inside the lines. She moves to the beat of her own drum, which is scary as an owner but also so refreshing. For example, I told her the CertifiKID business model is to send only one email each day—never more, never less. One day, she pushed back and said, "Why the hell can't I send out a second, "Last Chance" email for my deal?" She pushed and pushed me until I finally gave in. The next thing you know, we sold 500 more vouchers for that deal from that "Last Chance" email. Another example: a business would tell her to run a "Monday–Thursday only" offer, but she would make it "weekday only" and apologize later. No matter how many times she does this kind of stuff, NO ONE ever gets mad at her because her instincts and decisions are almost always spot on. They end up thanking her! Therefore, I give her quite a bit of slack to take risks with new opportunities and manage her key relationships, none of whom have ever called me with a complaint.

2. **Don't worry about the money.** Leslie never asked about money. She trusted that we would treat her fairly (and we certainly did, as she soon made a lot of money!), but the secret to her success is that she never makes money the priority. She always works in the best interest of the client and for the right reasons. This has led to her developing relationships with businesses that come back to her again and again, and makes her an incredible closer, as no business ever feels she is desperate for a deal.

3. **Ask a ton of questions before selling anything.** I have been on many sales calls with Leslie over the years, and the key to her success is her genuine interest in understanding the business and its needs. She pounds owners with questions about their businesses and comes up with deals that work best for them based on its short- or long-term strategy, as opposed to just trying to "sell" them on anything.

On the flip side, working with Leslie also has its challenges. She has always made it clear that she does not like following rules. In the early days, that worked. We were a small company and, as you saw in the above examples, sometimes bending the rules is beneficial. However, years later when we started professionalizing our business and infrastructure, Leslie's "no rules" approach became much more difficult to accommodate.

How do we keep our "secret weapon" happy when the only thing important to her is freedom? The best analogy I can think of is that Leslie is a racehorse (or diva) who has an immense amount of raw talent and doesn't like to be saddled or steered. She doesn't care about accolades but is in it for the thrill and wants to be free to race and run. So how do you manage and work with someone who you know can help your business and would be a waste to keep in the barn, who doesn't react well to being "managed," but who could also cause some collateral damage?

Here are the main lessons I learned in how to effectively manage a key employee who is also a friend, which can apply to any business that is trying to get the best out of a star on your team without burning the whole business down:

1. **Let her take the lead.** I learned over time to let Leslie feel like she is the one setting the terms. I never insisted that she participate in anything that was required of the rest of the team. I strongly encouraged her to do so or explained why it would be helpful to her and the team, as opposed to suggesting it was a requirement. I realized this was a risk, but she eventually evolved and accepted that she needed to adapt herself into the growing team dynamic and culture because she did not want to look like she was receiving special treatment or put me in an awkward position.

2. **Managing the friendship.** In all work environments, there are bound to be romances and special friendships that bloom. This is always tricky, and especially so when you own the business. Over the years, my friendship with Leslie has had its ups and downs. There was even one year where we basically stopped talking to each other, as she would constantly rub in my face that she was off at Six Flags enjoying her "I don't have to work

in the summers" schedule while I was working around the clock and pulling my hair out. However, we eventually reopened the lines of communication, promised each other we would always be honest about our feelings, and established some clarity regarding our respective expectations. Things improved as I grew the business and hired more people, which took the pressure off Leslie (and me) as being indispensable to the business's success. And once the pressure was off, Leslie started performing even better under her own initiative, as she liked the internal competition as much as the external competition. Our friendship and business relationship also evolved once Leslie understood how much weight I had on my shoulders, how many others on the team depended on the business, and that I needed her to act like my business partner as much as my friend or even employee. Our families are now incredibly close; I think my mom even hangs out with her more than she does with me.

Bien, our chief technology officer (CTO), was our next key addition to the CertifiKID team.

Let me back up and dive a bit deeper into the story about our original website developers that I mentioned earlier so you don't make the same mistakes that we did.

In January 2010, I hired a guy off Craigslist to build the original CertifiKID website. His site and portfolio looked amazing, his price was right, and he was local. Score! Or not . . .

A couple of months in, after repeatedly pushing for a status update with no response, I put my security background to work and did some digging. I found his Twitter page and saw pictures of him passed out on "Spring Break in Florida." Little did I know when I hired him that he was right out of college and his partner, who was the actual back-end developer, was still in college and living at home with his parents. Somehow the site was built (not well) and we got off the ground, but I quickly realized its shortcomings and knew we needed to significantly invest in the IT infrastructure and essentially start over from scratch.

Enter my hero, Bien. Bien was doing work for Brian's law firm when we hired him to rebuild and redesign the website. And he has been with us ever since. Not only is Bien amazing, devoted, and creative, he's also an incredible communicator, a rare find in a CTO!

When you find someone like this, count your blessings and do whatever it takes to keep that employee happy.

Amie, our chief operating officer (COO), was the next vital addition to our team. You will love this story. I remember being on the elliptical looking at my email when I saw a message inquiring about running a deal on the site and asking how everything works. But something about the email seemed sketchy to me, setting off my security background radar (sensing a theme here?). I Googled the email address and discovered it was linked to a girl named Amie. I Googled her name and saw that Amie was a Baltimore blogger who was all about deals. Aha! I caught this girl in the act trying to gather reconnaissance on my business!

I pushed her a bit in my response, and she came clean, admitting she was trying to find out more information about our business model because she was interested in starting a similar business. I think we tried to coordinate a meeting, but it didn't work out. A few months later, Amie applied for a position with CertifiKID. I put our prior weird exchange behind us and initially hired her for a sales position, but she quickly worked her way up the ladder. She's now our COO and runs the business's day-to-day operations. She's truly my right hand. Some people joke that it's the "Jamie and Amie show," which shows how much an impact she's had on our development and success. I could not imagine CertifiKID without her, as I often feel like she can read my mind!

Over the past decade, we've probably had over a hundred other team members come and go. However, the fact that we found such gems in Leslie, Bien, and Amie early on who remain our core leadership team to this day was essential.

The other major issue that became a challenge for us a few years in was that our salespeople were all working as non-salaried, commission-only independent contractors. The benefit of building a sales team this way was that there was little financial risk to the business if they didn't perform well. However, this led to us hiring new people left and right who were often gone a few weeks later if they were not generating sales. It was a huge investment of my personal time to onboard and train them and super frustrating when they often walked out the door without a word a few weeks later if the money didn't start flowing in immediately.

I pitched the sales role as the perfect job for a mom who wanted the best of both worlds—the flexibility to work from home on your own schedule and be present at your child's field trips. I had no problem getting interested candidates but struggled to get the medium- to long-term commitment that the position required to be successful. Looking back, I think this model was helpful for us to avoid risk as we built the business, but I also think it was a bit shortsighted because it proved challenging to manage. We likely also missed out on a lot of great opportunities by not having a truly committed sales team back then.

The unpredictable nature of the work also made it difficult to find and retain strong long-term candidates. You can work for weeks, or even months, to get a business to run a deal only to have the deal be a total bust. On the other hand, you can see a deal on Groupon, shoot the business owner an email, and have a deal up on the site within an hour and that ends up running year after year. I love the exhilaration of it all and the unknown, but not that many people are truly cut out for that high risk/high reward mentality. Former customers, and those who felt passionately about the business, were the ones who were best able to ride the wave and ended up thriving in the role.

Looking back on the team building and team managing side of starting and growing a business, I'd say this has been my greatest personal challenge. To be frank, I am not good at it and don't enjoy it. Between recruiting, onboarding, and training; making sure employees are happy with their responsibilities, compensation, and career growth; managing the issues that arise between employees (especially sales teams); and having to fire employees who aren't performing up to expectations, it's akin to listening to my least favorite music playlist where I keep skipping to the next song only to realize I don't like any of them.

It is simply a lot to manage and handle mentally every day, and not something I ever thought about when I came up with my business idea. I like being an entrepreneur and creating, conceiving, and executing. I don't enjoy managing people, and I don't like team drama. And, with a team of mainly outgoing and dynamic moms, we have had our share of team drama. However, in the end, the team is the most important part of the business and our greatest asset. Until you build it and can rely on it and get it right, you will never have time to focus on the truly important things, like the business vision and strategy, growth, new revenue models, new partnerships, and new markets.

Fortunately, it was also during this period that Brian agreed to step in and take the lead on all HR and personnel issues. He would speak regularly with all team members. He was also the last person to talk to every candidate we considered hiring, which was a great sanity check for me. He pushed us to organize quarterly team meetings at our house and led them, which was a huge load off my shoulders and allowed me to focus on managing day by day and pursuing key opportunities.

This all created some space between the team and me which he could uniquely fill. Where managing people is a challenge for me, it comes easy and is a strength for him. He has proven to be a key partner for me to achieve the right level of balance and perspective with all team members.

HE SAID: Your team (not you) is the most important asset of your business.

By year four, we were doing extremely well with sales and growing the business between ten to twenty percent each year, with very strong profitability.

Jamie could never get herself to believe the business was sustainable. She lived in a self-imposed alternate reality. Her dad and I would show her the numbers, I would show her the balance in the business account and what she was making from the business, but she didn't want to know and acted like she didn't care. (Remember, this is someone who can't even use an ATM.)

There would be nights where she would tell me in bed before we went to sleep that she thought the whole business could come crashing down the next day for one reason or another. I would try to comfort her that this risk was remote, but she didn't like my "glass is half full" thinking when hers was that the glass was "half empty." She would tell me (or yell at me, depending on the mood) that I wasn't close enough to what was happening and didn't understand. I'd eventually retreat and just assure her that if the business stopped operating tomorrow, it would be okay. We could pay the bills, pay our mortgage, and our lives wouldn't end.

In retrospect, I think this was her way of avoiding the pressure of feeling like, if the business failed, we would be losing everything and causing pain to our family—though this mindset does reflect Jamie's risk-averse and conservative nature, which informed many of our business and personal financial decisions during this period. On balance, I think this has served us well on both fronts, but there clearly were more risks we could have taken along the way that could have yielded bigger rewards sooner.

While growing our team, we still maintained a home office and virtual workplace. Most of our team members were still contractors and Jamie's dad, Gary, was working for poker money as our CFO. But we were hitting our stride and the business was becoming sustainable.

My challenge was convincing Jamie to invest more in our team, hire more, and delegate more. This was the first year we started to do it. As Jamie discusses, in this year we brought on board the people who would ultimately form our core leadership team (VP of sales, CTO, and COO), which has been key in helping us get to where we are today.

I missed the mark by pushing her to get a personal assistant to come to our home office every day. I wanted the assistant to do all of Jamie's administrative work, research, sales prospecting, and office organizing. But Jamie couldn't take the invasion of space; it made her feel guilty about exercising or leaving her desk for a banana, and she thought it was a waste of money. So multiple people didn't make it through this gauntlet before we ultimately gave up on this approach.

Good examples included the woman who posted a complaint about Jamie and her job on her Facebook page, obviously forgetting that Jamie was her Facebook friend and that she'd be seeing that lovely message in real time sitting five feet away. Another was on the phone taking personal calls 50 percent of the time in her office, jumping from one emergency to another. And another employee was in the middle of a toxic boyfriend relationship that brought her into the house every day in either a state of depression or fury. You get the picture.

It's a good lesson. Everyone works differently. I have worked mainly in traditional office and business settings and so have preconceived notions about what work and roles should be handled by which people and positions on a team. I tried to fit this traditional square peg into a nontraditional round hole. When it's your own business and you work virtually, we learned you must do what makes sense for you—and comfort and flexibility are key.

In our case, Jamie wanted to work in her own silo at home with all the support being virtual. It has its pros and cons, though ultimately she is most effective and happy working in this way. She also wanted to keep her hand on the wheel and micromanage certain areas, like sales. She has taken this approach until today, even as we have grown and evolved. It's not what they would teach in business school, or what you would hear from any "business experts," but it works for us and when it's your own business and you have all the control, you have the luxury of flipping traditional scripts and writing your own story the way you want.

When we hired new people at this stage of the business, we used a three-month probationary period for new hires, which gave us the comfort of bringing people on quickly even if we weren't 100 percent sure about them, as we could then part ways in a relatively short period if we didn't think that it was a good long-term fit. The problem was that Jamie had such high standards that few made it through the period, so it became a revolving door, especially on the sales side, which can be an internal administrative drain.

But in addition to our leadership team, we brought on board many team members in this period who are still with us or had very long runs.

Why did some go the distance? As Jamie also explains, we think the common ingredient was that they were passionate about our business—being a resource for parents and moms to find local experiences outside the home at great values to make memories with their kids. So where did these people come from? Our subscribers, of course.

Jamie would send out an email to our subscribers and always got many inquiries from loyal followers who knew and loved the essence of our business. Many of them were moms who stopped working outside the home to raise their kids and didn't think that a virtual opportunity where you could have flexibility with your schedule, financial upside, and passion for what you were doing even existed. Most of our team members thus came from our subscriber list or a referral from a subscriber, or a business partner, or from our space. And these people came with passion for who we are and what we do. It wasn't just a job. It was joining our family and serving their community.

Of course, it didn't always work out. I handled most of the termination calls, which were all by phone as this was pre-Zoom. I'd get advice from our external employment counsel regarding the message and we would script ourselves so the calls would be short and sweet, which is an approach I'd recommend. Naturally, they don't all go that way, so you need to be prepared and anticipate the employee's questions and responses. For example, "Can I have another chance?" or "I was never trained to be successful in my position" or "Your expectations are too high" or "My performance has been affected by my personal issues" or "Why are you treating me differently than [EMPLOYEE X]?" and on and on.

My stock response to all of these questions or feedback when you have made the decision to separate, which was a great suggestion from my employment counsel and always seems to work, is this: "We have considered all of the issues and feel it just is not the right fit. We do not feel it would be helpful to get more into the weeds or details on this call as we have unfortunately made our decision. We wish you well. Take care. Goodbye."

I know this sounds harsh and too short, but consider that it follows the employee's airing of their response to the decision. The employee often wants specific examples in these situations—to know what was the straw that broke the camel's back—but rarely is it one thing, which is never satisfactory from the employee's perspective. Therefore, the key is that, as the employer in an at-will arrangement, you do not need, nor will it serve either party to have, a wide-ranging discussion about "why" the decision was made. Be honest, direct, speak at a high level if possible, and most importantly, keep it short.

The irony with the "keep it short" mantra is that I am notoriously long-winded. I always have been. Brevity has never been a strength. Ask my colleagues at my firm and with the business. Ask my kids. Ask Jamie. Though Jamie rarely makes a big deal of it, which I appreciate. Because she is the opposite, I think she feels I am often trying to compensate for her not being a "talker" or, to put it another way, "BS-er." I've tried to work on this shortcoming over the years and it's still a battle, though I do think running a business has helped, as has trying to balance the business with my legal practice. You simply don't have the time to dive too deeply into issues and your team needs direction in real time.

I'm also not a quick decision-maker. Again, ask those close to me and they'll be nodding their heads. I like to hear all sides and reach a consensus solution. And I'm good at finding solutions that, as I like to say, everyone is uncomfortably comfortable with. This area is another good example of how Jamie and I balance each other. She's a quick decision-maker and is always pushing me to keep up with her on issues.

While it often feels to her like I am slowing everyone down, I think she appreciates the thoughtful sanity check I provide on big and small decisions, especially ones related to our team. As you heard from her, she doesn't like dealing with team conflicts and doesn't feel she is good at it either. It's also a big distraction from her vital work of managing and growing our business. In other words, she likes being an entrepreneur first, and a CEO and manager second. I don't necessarily like dealing with conflicts—who does—but it's a strength for me and I've had lots of experience in mediation and disputes, so I feel I can be objective and gain trust from both sides. But this work is time consuming, emotional, and exhausting—which is a strain for owners who also are trying to raise a family.

The lesson is that you need to find someone on your team to provide balance to your weaknesses. And it doesn't have to be the same person for every area. For example, maybe someone is ideal for taking the lead on hiring, but another person is better at firing. Maybe someone is better at working fast and efficiently, but make sure they are teamed with someone who is very detail oriented. The goal is to be well rounded and have your bases covered. This was our goal in this period as we were building a team to last and help us grow our business in smart, effective, and sustainable ways.

WE SAY: Hire people who are passionate about your business.

When we think back over the years, we probably have spent 80 percent of our time discussing and managing employee and team issues. When you make it and need a real team, it ends up being the biggest priority. As much as you want to focus on the entrepreneurial side of it all, in the end you must build, maintain, and lead a team that sees your vision and can execute it. Our strongest and most long-standing employees over time have been the ones with a true passion for our business and their work. It's so simple and basic, but also so true.

YEAR 5

The Messy Middle

**SHE SAID: Take care of yourself first,
then worry about everything (and everyone) else.**

When I found out Oprah was coming to town for a two-day "Live Your Best Life" weekend seminar, I pounced at the chance to attend with my friend Carol. At this two-day conference, Oprah had us take a deep dive into our lives. I found myself inspired many times throughout the event but there was one assignment that really hit home with me. Oprah asked us to take out our workbooks where there was a giant empty circle. She had us divide the circle into pieces of pie based on the way our life was currently divided, with the different slivers representing time devoted to children/family, spouse, exercise, friends, work, spirituality, hobbies/interests, etc.

When I looked down at my completed pie, I realized how out of whack my life had become. My children and my work basically took up my entire pie. Everything else was a tiny sliver. The point of the exercise was to see how we currently live versus how we would like to live. I left that day knowing I needed to make some changes in my life.

The first thing I did was sign up for yoga. I had tried yoga with my sister years before and almost got kicked out because we spent the whole class giggling. We could not take it seriously. This time was different. I found a yoga studio that was in my neighborhood, which was yoga on steroids, and it challenged me like I had never been challenged before, both physically and mentally. I pushed myself to go to yoga religiously from that day on and have never looked back. It gave me an outlet I needed.

I convinced Brian to come with me one time, and somehow, he fought through the insecurity of being the only guy in the class and ended up getting really into it as well. In the years since, yoga has become an amazing activity that we do together to relieve stress and get a good workout. It has paid big dividends for our physical and mental health.

The next lesson I took from the session with Oprah was realizing the enormous amount of mom guilt I had been carrying around all these years and the impact it was having on my daily routine, choices, and mental state. All these years I had refused to get any additional support, such as a nanny, babysitter, or housekeeper, despite Brian's regular pleas. Looking back, I am not sure why I felt this way, but I know it had to do with mom guilt or perhaps, mom fear. I know many other moms must have these same feelings. I don't think I have really outgrown this mentality, but my kids are now at an age where I don't need the help.

Just acknowledging the guilt for the first time was cathartic for me. I had put pressure on myself to make sure I did not miss a beat as a mom. It was like I had made a pact with myself that if I was going to spend all this time on my business, which was time I could be spending with them, I'd be around and there for everything. But it was hard and always a race. I realized I just needed to do my best and make sure my pie was getting filled up appropriately, so I was in a good place for them.

I also spent a lot of time that weekend thinking about my relationship with Brian, where we were at and where we had come from.

I was feeling a sense of loss, the loss of time for intimacy and connection as a couple, given the demands of our business and kids.

To give you a sense of what our typical day looked like back then, we both woke up between 6:00 and 7:00 a.m. (unless Brian was in another country on work travel, which was 25 percent of the time). I rolled out of bed and immediately grabbed my phone to see what I'd missed overnight. Typically, there were already things I needed to jump on as I pounded away on my iPhone from the toilet. I got myself together, which meant throwing on my running clothes, brushing my teeth, and putting my hair in a ponytail; made my favorite coffee; and went right to my computer to pound away as much as possible before the kids woke up. I got their lunch prepared, made sure there were no forms I needed to sign, and then woke up the kids and helped them get ready for their day.

I took the kids to school or to the bus stop, trying hard to focus on them and not on my phone but probably still checking it as often as I could to make sure I was not missing anything. Once I got them off, I was all business. I had six hours of solid working time to get as much shit done as possible. Somehow in those six hours, I always made sure to get my one-hour run in. When my workday was over, I'd grab the kids and head to their afternoon activities, which typically involved soccer. My laptop came along with me wherever I went, and I'd park myself and crank away. After activities, we would grab takeout on the way home, and then I'd get the kids started on their homework, showered, and in bed. Phew.

Brian usually arrived home after I had finally settled the kids for bed and would inevitably wind them back up again. He would then start cleaning up after me—the kitchen counters, the table, the floors, dishes, laundry, and so on. I waited for him on the couch where the second portion of his workday would begin with CertifiKID—around 9:00 p.m. I constantly told him I felt like his secretary at this point of the day, queuing up everything he needed. I also felt frustrated half the time because he seemed elsewhere and not in the moment.

We worked, while half-watching some sort of TV show, and I would go through the list of what we needed to tackle and vent to him about what had occurred during my day. Around 11:00 p.m., I'd usually hit my limit and head up to bed where I'd quickly pass out. Brian would join me at some point (usually without me knowing it) after finishing both what he needed to do for me, and his law firm work. That was our world!

With a schedule like that, Brian's energy was limited and I was tired, so it was a struggle to find any time for us to relax and enjoy time together. There was also built-up frustration. I realized it was time for us to make our marriage a priority, starting with a trip alone to Sedona, Arizona, for our tenth anniversary. Of course, the trip still included our laptops and plenty of strategic talks about business on hikes, but there was also plenty of time for fun and connection and meals where we put our phones away and just relaxed. Yoga. Green smoothies. Clean air. Spa time. When we got home, I think we both realized how important that time was, and we needed to make it a priority in the future to have time together.

A few months later, as I was trying to get my life more in balance, an opportunity came to us that both tested us and our commitment to the future of the company. Our biggest competitor outside of Groupon at the time was a company called Plum District. They launched about a month after we did and were backed by venture capital financing. Therefore, they had loads of cash to put into their business and help them expand their team and national reach. They employed moms all over the country to get deals and were doing an incredible job. At one point, they even used celebrities like Soleil Moon Frye (ask Punky Brewster) and Bethenny Frankel to endorse and advise them. They were big time in my eyes!

Remember that DoodleDeals company that tried to buy us? Well, about a year after they approached us, they were acquired by Plum District. More evidence to support the theory that the best deals are sometimes those you don't do, right? I had kept in touch with the DoodleDeals' founder, so I reached out to him to check in and inquire about the Plum District acquisition. He, in turn, introduced me to the new CEO of Plum District, a powerhouse executive they brought over from Google.

When I shared the name of the new CEO with Brian, he had a puzzled look on his face and asked me to pull her up on LinkedIn. When he saw her profile, he gasped. Brian and the CEO had gone to the same high school in the Pittsburgh area. Not only that, but they were friends; Brian had been senior class president and she had been vice president. No freakin' way, right?

So, Brian called up his old pal to try to get the scoop. It became clear that the reason she was brought in was to get the business in a position to sell, which essentially entailed taking measures to get them in the black as quickly as possible, and to then solicit and entertain offers and see through any potential transaction.

They had a few active suitors, and one that was particularly aggressive. The CEO was not sold on their vision for the company, though their price was right. After discussions with us, she indicated that the synergy with CertifiKID would be ideal if we could at least come somewhere close to the other company's price and could make an offer quickly. She asked if we would be interested in the opportunity.

WOW.

This was the opportunity that we needed to finally scale the business nationally, but were we willing to go from a profitable business to potentially investing and risking millions of dollars with this acquisition? Was I willing to take on and integrate an entire new team of employees and absorb all the associated pressure? Was I willing to throw the balance off again that I had been trying to achieve this past year on a personal front?

Brian and I talked . . . and talked . . . and talked about it. The answer was "YES!" We decided it was worth taking this huge financial and personal risk to take the business to the next level. We spoke to the CEO, and she suggested that, if we offered a certain price, she would recommend to her board that they accept our offer. We got our bankers and external legal counsel involved (our legal counsel, Doug, is Brian's good buddy who also went to the same high school and knew the CEO!) and put together and submitted a formal offer that was very close to (but not exactly) what she suggested. Brian said it is a negotiation after all and it was a lot of money. We held our breath.

A week went by with no news. Then another week. This was not good. We eventually found out they went with the other company. We assume our offer helped the CEO seal the deal for them and got them better final terms. We got played. I was disappointed but also a tiny bit relieved since we were finally getting to this more balanced lifestyle I was after, which would have been torn to shreds. Not to mention the stress this investment and risk would have caused me.

Now my fear moved to this new buyer and the competition it would stir up. The crazy part is that nothing ever materialized in terms of increased competition from Plum District after this transaction. The new buyer relaunched the company and then it seemed to fizzle, as far as we could tell, in the mom-deal space. Thus, it worked out in the end because our biggest competitor was out of the picture, though to this day, I wonder what we could have done with all their assets and reach.

Even though we did not make this acquisition, I do think this opportunity tested us by helping us understand how serious we were with our business, how far we were willing to go, and what risks we were willing to take to grow and get to the next level. We had many experiences like this over the decade and each one was a huge learning experience. Despite all the emotions, time, and effort that go into these kinds of opportunities, there is a great amount to learn and grow from, so it is never a regret.

In the end, this probably falls under the adage that some of God's greatest gifts are unanswered prayers. In business, there are many of these.

**HE SAID: Don't talk shop while half-asleep
in bed binge-watching your favorite TV show.**

I never used to be a neat freak. My mom waited on me hand and foot. She still can't believe how obsessed with cleanliness I have become. But marrying a slob has a way of making you Mr. Clean. #sorrynotsorry. Throw messy kids and the demands of the business in the mix, and I was in a perpetual state of being on edge. But I learned long ago never to make comments. I'd just clean up after Jamie—the open Splenda packs lying around everywhere, dirty rags, spills that weren't cleaned up, a new concoction or mixer being tried every day.

And with the business, it was the same thing—lots of spills not cleaned up and nothing organized or put away. I pushed . . . and pushed . . . for Jamie to get a personal assistant to come to the house and help with the business. She fought this for years, but finally gave in. She HATED having someone in the house and in her space, so those adventures were short-lived. I suggested a housekeeper or nanny instead. "Nope, waste of money. My parents never had a cleaning lady." I pushed for more help with the kids. "Nope, waste of money. We don't need it. I'm home all day, so this is a benefit." Still on edge . . .

By year five, or as we like to call it, "the messy middle," we were dealing with how to co-parent kids who now required different kinds of attention and couldn't be put in a stroller or pacified by a game of hide-and-seek. And Jamie was resisting and then refusing to get any additional help (#controlfreak). Every time I'd raise it, she'd scowl at me, and I'd crawl back in my hole.

Jamie chose the alternative, which was to work around the clock, and with the benefit of working at home, her compromise was that she would also prioritize the kids by taking them to and from the bus, hosting playdates, being their chauffeur, and helping them with homework, even if she couldn't volunteer at their school or chaperone a field trip. She'd take calls in her minivan, carry her laptop to practices, and work until midnight to get it all done.

I'd try to stay out of the way—which was easy because I was usually either at the office or traveling—and just make sure I was getting through Jamie's list even if I was struggling with being in the moment or making eye contact. My bandwidth was just not enough for it all, but as long as I completed her list!—which she always wanted me to do late at night in bed when we were finally getting our hour of downtime to watch our latest favorite TV series (i.e., *Mad Men* or *Breaking Bad*). My eyes would glaze over, the words would go in one ear and out the other. Finally, I begged her not to talk shop after 10:00 p.m. She occasionally accommodated.

Our tenth anniversary trip to Sedona was something we both desperately needed. I tried practicing yoga there for the first time, which proved transformative as, once we got back home, Jamie took me to her local yoga studio and I tried it again with her. I was one of only two guys in a class of twenty. Even though everyone was smiley and friendly, they were giving me a look of pity as if I were a lamb headed for slaughter. And boy was I slaughtered.

Even though I considered myself reasonably flexible for a guy my age and felt in decent shape, I was moving muscles I hadn't ever moved. As the newbie, I was the teacher's (who happened to be the owner) pet for the class, and he kept adjusting me and putting extra pressure on me. I was wincing, moaning, and groaning through the whole class. It was not enjoyable. After barely making it through, I limped out and was in such pain the next day that I didn't think I'd ever go back.

But then, when Jamie said she was going again, I said I'd try it one more time. The owner was happy to see me and paid a lot of attention to me again during the class, but I did better. I also found myself drawn to the breathing techniques and really enjoyed the wind down at the end where you just lie on the mat and breathe.

I soon got into the habit of going a few times a week and felt my physical and mental health improving. I got stronger. My balance and flexibility improved, and I gained confidence. I'd push myself and do something in a class that I never thought I could do in a previous class, like a handstand. I also would bask in the final fifteen minutes of "Savasana" where control of breath, mind, and body are released. Of course, Jamie would always want to leave early and hated Savasana. She felt it was a waste of time and would spend the fifteen minutes stressing about what was on her to-do list. This difference between us speaks for itself, doesn't it?

I also really enjoyed practicing with Jamie. We were one of the very few couples that practiced together, and it was a special time where we could be together but focus on our own individual well-being. We have continued to practice yoga together for the most part since, though we have had some droughts. Finding this kind of outlet is important to achieve work-life balance, but having it be an outlet for you to do alone as well as in your marriage or partnership is obviously an extra bonus.

Despite the day-to-day hustle and bustle, the business was growing, and we were becoming very profitable. This helped drive some further hiring with our operations and sales teams. Also, opportunities seemed to be coming our way, such as the Plum District opportunity.

Most companies that are generating the kind of sales that we were at this time, which was millions in annual sales, would take formal approaches to scaling. For example, they would look to private equity to secure additional funding or brokers to create acquisition opportunities. We never took these approaches. The reason? We were profitable, had no debt, and didn't want to lose control or extend ourselves beyond our capacity. And we were prepared to extend ourselves in terms of our own investment and risk, as we were already essentially reinvesting profits in the business.

Thus, when I had the chance to talk to my former high school classmate about Plum District, we had the luxury of not needing to get approval to make an offer or seek capital contributions from investors. We just had to decide if we were prepared to make the investment. It was a LOT of money for us to consider and, while we had the cash, I secured a credit line guaranteed by our house just to test if that would be better from a money management perspective.

My classmate was a straight shooter and said to me, if you make an offer at this level, I'll recommend that the board accept it. She felt we would be better caretakers of the business than the other potential buyer, who was quite advanced with them and had put considerably more money on the table than what she suggested to me we would need to offer.

Jamie and I took many walks trying to decide what to do. We went around and around. We landed on the fact that this was our best chance yet to take our business to the next level and potentially steal this company that had started with $20 million in VC financing. We decided to take our shot but to make an offer we were comfortable with to throw our hat in the ring and if we didn't get it, it wasn't meant to be.

Because this did feel like a negotiation and we weren't convinced the cash element was worth what she suggested, we ultimately decided to offer 15 percent less than my classmate's suggestion. My sense was that if that last 15 percent was so important, she would have come back and encouraged us to top it up to get to that number. But we never got the chance. We made our formal LOI (letter of intent) proposal and heard crickets. Finally, three weeks later, I chased her, and she said they had gone with the original buyer. Jamie felt we had been played. I wasn't so sure.

Like all negotiations that don't result in a deal, I had some sleepless nights second-guessing myself. Had we been penny wise and pound foolish? What if we had offered EXACTLY what she asked for? Would she have delivered? By not doing so, did we make it impossible for her to treat it as a serious proposal with her board? Or was Jamie right that she used our offer to extract the final concessions she needed from the other buyer to consummate their deal? I think she may very well be right, but we'll never know.

We were bummed for about a day. I'd equate our feelings to putting an offer on a house that you would love to have but the price is probably higher than what the house is worth. So, when your offer "under ask" is rejected and you don't get the house, you feel more relief than disappointment.

And we learned from the process and experience. We were satisfied that we had analyzed the opportunity critically, made a legitimate proposal we were comfortable with, and put our best foot forward. We also learned several lessons in the process:

1. **We would "go for it" if the right opportunity presented itself.**
2. **When making any proposal, make sure you are comfortable with it and will have no regrets if you get the deal.**
3. **Sometimes the best deals are ones you don't get.**

Like the DoodleDeals opportunity, I think the trajectory of our entire business would have changed if we had gotten the Plum District deal, and not in a good way. The investment was in a depreciating asset and would have put pressure on Jamie to get a return on it. We were not equipped at that time to take that business over and integrate it into ours.

They were one of our biggest competitors and, ultimately, their sale to the other buyer took them out of our space, so it worked out well for us in that way. And it would have all gotten even messier, and no amount of yoga would have salvaged whatever work-life balance we were trying to achieve.

**WE SAY: Find something outside the business
and kids that you can do together to relieve stress.**

How we made it through these messy years is hard to fathom and the fact that we were worried about balance and hitting all the marks is honestly ridiculous. Just take care of yourself, find an outlet outside of the business to do together, and survive. We know there are all these expectations of what life should look like through social media and society, but who gives a shit? If you can manage a business and get through the early child-rearing years in one piece, you get a 10/10 in our book!

· 6 ·

YEAR 6
What's Success Got To Do With It?

**SHE SAID: Once you embrace the success
you have achieved, others will see you as a success.**

After going through the process with the Plum District opportunity and seeing where we could take this business, we realized we needed to professionalize ourselves. It was time. Up until this point, it often felt like we were in the wild west. Even though we had a strong core team, I had my foot in every piece of the business and needed to finally start to take my hands off the wheel.

I was still setting up and sending the daily emails to our subscribers with the featured deal because I was too nervous to let anyone else take over. I was still doing a large portion of the sales. I also did most of the administrative work because I always found it easier to do it myself than to ask for help. I took care of all the logistics for our team meetings, which included ordering food and gifts. The list goes on and on. I could not help myself. I am a doer, impatient, and don't have time for BS.

Brian would push me every day about how much of the sales I was still doing. I was good at it and loved it. He told me it was nuts, for example, that I was still dealing with "The Great Zucchini" and the owner of a local basketball camp who would text me on a Saturday night to make changes to his deal. He said I should also not be perceived by my sales staff to be competing with them in any respect for new leads.

However, on the flip side, when sales were down, he would push me to jump back in and start getting revenue up to give us a jolt. So, I would go back and forth, which wasn't ideal. I began shifting in the direction of really trying to pull away from sales while keeping my toes

My approach today is to try to stay out of doing the actual sales work as much as possible for the benefit of the team dynamic. I encourage this, so—do as I say now, not as I have done.

in the water, so I'd have a pulse on our markets and could stay sharp and on trend.

It was time to get our acts together in many respects. I needed more control over the team, especially the sales team, who seemed to think working in the summer was optional and second priority to days at the pool. It was at this point that we decided we needed to shift many on our team from being commission-only, independent contractors to W-2 salaried employees. We also introduced a benefits program for the first time. I could now start instituting real rules, expectations, and goals.

I will never forget when we rolled out to our team this new approach. We held an overnight company retreat every fall, and this particular year I decided it would be fun to rent out my old summer camp for the occasion. Let's just say the choice was not met with excitement. We had always held our retreat at a very nice hotel, and the team was looking forward to another five-star (or at least four-star!) experience, which this clearly was not. For starters, the camp is Jewish, so the food was all kosher. Need I say more? I also thought the location would really allow for team bonding in the casual and rustic environment, close quarters, and isolated location. Um, no.

The morning everyone arrived, Brian and I went through the new company policies and structural changes. Our presentation was met with literal tears from some of the women. What was I doing to these moms who wanted to be able to go on every single field trip, extended holidays, and summer sabbaticals? It was as if I was ruining their lives, and they didn't like that it was presented as take it or leave it, so they were confronted with deciding whether to stay with the company or run for the hills.

In the end, we allowed a part-time W-2 option to accommodate several of the more tenured and dedicated team members who I think were dealing with too much of their own mom guilt (but I couldn't judge considering I certainly had my own issues). We didn't lose any of the team on account of these changes and I think they all ultimately appreciated the salaries and benefits package. But it wasn't an easy transition.

In addition to this being the year we professionalized the business, it also was the year I became legitimized in the eyes of others. Up until this point, if you had asked most of the people who knew me at the preschool or from the neighborhood, they would tell you I was basically a stay-at-home mom who had a side mommy business, despite the fact I always had my laptop attached to me in every carpool line or on every soccer sideline.

I am a very quiet and introverted person, so unless you asked me specific questions about the business, I was not one who would say much or give details of the size or scope of what I was doing. That all changed when the *Washington Post* published a featured article on me on the front page of the Business section written by their well-known business reporter Thomas Heath.

Everyone always asks me how this came to be, so let me take you back to 2010 when I was just getting started. After a lot of research, I made myself a list of press contacts and sent out a blanket press release (using a template I found on Google) about the launch of my business. I noticed there was a reporter who was doing regular updates on LivingSocial named Thomas Heath ("Tom"), so I wrote him a personal email asking to be featured. I got a bite from him, and he told me to give him a call. That was the start to my offbeat relationship with my "boyfriend reporter" Tom.

Over the years to come, I would check in monthly with Tom. I would get a five-word email from him telling me to ping him at noon, and I would jump. Our calls were short and sweet and mainly consisted of him barking at me and cajoling me for information. I never actually met Tom in person, but he was an "old school" reporter and a bit of a curmudgeon. I gave him scoops on the daily deal market. I even went to a national Daily Deal conference and gave him my notes. And I gave him ideas for features on other entrepreneurs, given I was working with so many cool, local businesses (and they were all grateful if he ran a story on them).

He made me feel like the more I gave, the more he would reciprocate and write about CertifiKID. So that's what I did—I continued to give, and he kept to his word and threw me bones left and right. He gave me my first full feature in 2011, which was a game changer for me from a business perspective because it provided us with legitimacy in the eyes of many businesses who then took a chance with us by running a deal. Also, that first story was in the edition where the *Post* reported on the killing of Osama bin Laden, which happened the night before, so needless to say, it was very widely read.

Tom was all about the "numbers." He would push me to reveal details, and sometimes I would. Mostly I would tell him to talk to Brian, which led to them developing a funny relationship of their own. Brian was a tougher nut to crack and had experience with journalists like Tom, so Tom's "charm" and approach didn't work the same way with Brian, which frustrated Tom. Tom would often call me and complain about my "pain in the ass" husband. But Tom knew Brian was the gatekeeper of the numbers, which was the key ingredient for his stories, so his persistence with him and unwillingness to take no for an answer would often get him the goods he was looking for.

Tom was always curious to know what kind of car I was driving, and each time I would tell him about my minivan. He could not believe I had not upgraded, but I loved my minivan and was never into flashy brands. And a minivan was the perfect car for a mom. Not to mention that I am not a particularly good driver and don't want the pressure of a fancy car.

Knowing that the money and numbers were what got Tom excited about writing an article, I am not sure exactly what I told him, but in 2015, he decided to do another big story on us. He made me feel like a boyfriend does when he gives you a big gift. He never does a second story about an entrepreneur, and would be breaking his rule by doing so, so I was over the moon. Whether it was our relationship, my persistence, our growth and strong numbers, or the local LivingSocial dynamic (which at that time was the largest private employer in Washington, DC, and run by the *Post*'s publisher's son-in-law), it happened.

Honestly, I felt the timing couldn't have been better for the business. When the story ran, my phone blew up. Every friend, neighbor, and parent at my kids' school saw the story and said something to me about it, such as "I had no idea this was a real business" or "I thought you were a stay-at-home mom?" or "How have you been doing this under the radar?" My parents and in-laws' friends were getting calls left and right too. It was a combination of shock, effusive praise, and celebrity treatment. They looked at me differently, especially the husbands who suddenly were interested in what I had to say as a serious business owner and equal and not just another stay-at-home mom. It was both strange and validating.

Over the course of this journey, every time I have started to lose my mojo, something major has happened to bring me back into the game. This was one of those points. The story explained the evolution of the business and why we were succeeding while others had failed. It included our sales numbers ($5 million at that point), which really blew people's minds because there are many successful businesses that never hit these kinds of numbers. Maybe I needed to see my story in print to truly appreciate what I had accomplished.

And if you're wondering about my current relationship with my boyfriend reporter Tom, he has now retired. But he still occasionally emails me, asks when I'm selling, and always makes sure to mention that I should give him an interest in my company for all he did to help put me on the map.

With success also came money. I have a very weird relationship with money. I grew up in a classic middle-class home with parents who often made it seem like we were living on food stamps, which made me hyper-focused on pinching pennies at a young age. It won't surprise you that my favorite clothing store was called Frugal Fannie's. My father was a government employee, and my mom was a teacher, so they were able to support us fine. But they constantly made clear that we could only have what we needed versus what we wanted.

Because I knew I wouldn't get any charity from them, I was constantly fixated on how I could get the items the other kids had or do the fun activities they were doing on my own. For example, I spent a lot of time trying to win prizes on the local AM radio station so our family could do dinners out, regardless of where (e.g., the bad Chinese or average chain restaurant); go to movies, regardless of which one (e.g., R-rated horror movie); or take trips, regardless of the time, destination, or catch (e.g., a Honeymoon suite with a bottle of champagne on a school night).

My family was obsessed with the "Entertainment Book" and my sister and I were hooked on a book called "Free Stuff for Kids," where we would write letters to random associations with the hope that they would send us a set of pencils. For college, my parents said they would pay for an instate school, but if we went somewhere else, we'd have to pay the difference. Of course, my sister chose the instate school, and I chose the out-of-state school, which meant I had a tab with my dad well after grad school, though this motivated me to finish college a semester early so I could more quickly get to the point where I had a decent paying job and could start paying that tab back! It was quite a satisfying day for both my dad and me when I sent him the last payment and knew I was in the black!

I do believe this mentality served me well when it came to being an entrepreneur. However, when I started making money, I struggled with it, as strange as that sounds—though during this period, I did treat myself to a Starbucks Frappuccino virtually every day. I still had this voice in my head telling me "it's not necessary" and "there has to be a less expensive option" on everything, big and small.

I also feel a real high when I get a good deal, like my $1,000 Vera Wang wedding dress that I sold on eBay the day after my wedding for a profit. Meanwhile, I don't get any sort of high when I buy a new purse or even a new house. Brian bought me diamond earrings and I had to rationalize it to myself that I will leave those earrings in my ears for thirty years, never take them out, and not buy other earrings, so "they make sense."

I always dreamed that I would know I was rich when I was doing my regular weekly grocery shopping at Whole Foods. I could never imagine how anyone could spend $12 on a single container of guacamole. Occasionally, now, I do grab an item I need at Whole Foods, but I *still* to this day do not feel I am at the point psychologically where I can load up my cart with groceries there. I wonder if it's possible one day, if I ever sold my business. In the end, I don't know if I will *ever* get over this complex of mine. I think it may be too entrenched in my brain alongside my fear that one day all the money will be gone and all I will think about is the $12 I wasted on that damn guacamole.

To be fair, I have learned to let it go a bit. I have felt the benefits and advantages of having money. For example, when my kids want to do activities like go to sleepaway camp during the summer, I don't think twice. I know how out-of-reach and difficult this concept must be for some parents to shell out all this money, plus then they have to buy their kids all the gear that comes with it every year, not to mention the transportation and visiting day costs. It is absurd. But it is a relief not to have to worry if we can keep doing it every year. It feels good to give my kids an incredible experience that carries them through the school year and allows them to make lifelong friendships with kids from all over the country.

Ultimately, I look at the money I have earned from my success as freedom. I always made most of my decisions around money. What I would wear, do each day, choose for a career, decide to do for a trip, etc. I was always trying to find what would make the most sense financially regardless of what I could afford at that stage of my life. Having money finally gives me the freedom to make choices based on what I truly want and need in my life (as long as I ignore that voice that still rings in my head). It feels good.

And it probably all makes sense now that I started a DEAL business!

HE SAID: When you want to truly grow and be taken seriously, there's a point where you must stop acting like a mom-and-pop shop.

This is the point when we could finally breathe because we had hired people to handle most of the major roles, from operations to sales to marketing to customer service.

We had a COO (Amie) who was managing the daily operations and a director of customer experience (Randi) who was managing our customer service issues and communications. We had a director of marketing (Kim) who was more of a drill sergeant than Jamie was and focused on our advertising, marketing, and social media strategy. And we had full-time internal administration and operations support (Olga). All rockstars. Jamie didn't know what to do with herself. Bliss.

We started to see the impact of the foundation built over the years of thousands of families with whom we had worked, business owners with whom we'd built relationships, and all the employees and their families who had grown loyal and dedicated to our business and become like our extended family.

Our numbers were going through the roof—millions in sales and a growing list of hundreds of thousands of subscribers. While still fatigued, Jamie wasn't fatalistic about the business anymore.

She was hopeful.

She was also frustrated that we weren't doing even better than we were doing, given our opportunities, especially when summer rolled around. She attributed this to the seasonal and laissez-faire attitude of our sales team, and overreliance on Leslie. Jamie would see a business we had been trying to do a deal with for months run on another site and explode that we hadn't gotten them first.

To give you a sense of the conversation, July 4th would roll around, and this would be the weekly discussion:

JAMIE: What's the point of paying people if they can come and go as they please and take the whole summer off?

ME: Well, it's kind of the benefit for them of the 1099 structure. Why do you think they aren't working?

JAMIE: Look at the awful numbers! We are screwing ourselves for September and they will complain about their $20 monthly check, but this is why. Why are these moms not getting this?

ME: They don't need this job, it's a second income, and they want to spend time with their kids. So, let's just hire some full-time people so you don't have to rely on part-timers.

JAMIE: Why would we do that when this business could go down tomorrow? I'm just going to spend this whole week making calls and getting deals. I've been trying to get away from sales, but someone has to do it!

ME: Sigh.

If it wasn't clear before, Jamie is hyper-competitive from a business sense, which is somewhat ironic given she was never competitive from a traditional sports perspective and didn't care if her team won or lost. I think the point is that Jamie doesn't have an edge when she is part of a team of equals, but when she is the leader or the owner, she has the sharpest of edges. It's her money and she doesn't like to ever feel someone is taking advantage of her or wasting her money. You can probably understand this now that you have heard about her difficult relationship with money.

She would spend time and emotional energy obsessing whether people were working their hours, which was difficult enough to monitor in a remote workplace; and she'd micromanage certain client relationships when she felt balls were dropped or opportunities were not pursued. Of course, my challenge was explaining to her daily that if we had a 1099 relationship with someone, the whole point was they were an independent contractor and thus we couldn't dictate their schedules or hours in the same way.

It finally got to the point where she had enough confidence in the revenue the business was generating that she was prepared to convert our sales team members to W-2 employees. The tradeoff was that she would get a more engaged and accountable workforce, but we would have to pay larger salaries and offer a health and retirement benefits package. The strategy was that the additional cost would pay for itself but also increase the business's overall revenue, so everyone would be better off.

As Jamie explained, this was a difficult transition for many on our team who loved the flexibility of being stay-at-home moms who could work when they wanted and make money when they succeeded on a commission basis. Plus, we didn't give them an option. Therefore, it was quite a tough adjustment for some. But everyone ultimately stayed with us despite the status changes and after the first year, the analysis showed that most everyone was better off. And the business was a bit better off as well from everyone's extra focus and effort, though the real key was that we laid the foundation with the new structure which was necessary to go into the next phase of the business where we hoped to grow.

Another aspect of this change was that it required us to professionalize our internal structure from an HR perspective. This meant that I needed to step into this role and take the lead on handling these issues with everyone on the team. I would schedule quarterly calls with each team member, listen to their concerns, and provide any constructive feedback that we had for them in terms of their performance. Jamie would make lists of all the points she'd want to make to every employee and expect me to tackle them in these sessions with my personal touch. I'd also be the main communicator to the team generally on all benefits, compensation, and employment issues.

I think these shifts were integral to Jamie's development as CEO. They freed her to rely on her team more, delegate to a core management team, take the hand off the wheel a bit, and focus on the bigger strategy and opportunities of the business. Instead of constantly being in survival mode (or bitch mode), she was in a "build" mode. She focused 100 percent effort on adding that extra 10 percent of creativity or energy across the full range of what we were doing that would make all the difference. This is why we saw our best performance yet on deals during this period, like a $25,000 paid advertising fee, or selling 5,000 tickets to an event or 500 getaways to Great Wolf Lodge.

We hit $5 million in gross sales in this year alone (not something many businesses could ever say they achieved), and between her salary and business net income, Jamie was a millionaire. When I tried to talk to her about this milestone or finance issues generally, of course she didn't want to know, and didn't care. I'd get the canned retort: "This business could die tomorrow." Sigh.

But she finally let us reward ourselves by buying a small beach place three hours to the shore from our area where we have vacationed for years and always talked about buying something. We both love the beach—just being on the water, the air, the vibe. Some people love cities. Some people love the mountains. Some people love lakes. Some people love the desert. We like to visit these places but, as a unit, we love the beach the most and would stay there all year if we could. Jamie jokes that once the kids are off to college, we are downsizing and moving south to a beach because she HATES the cold and the winter.

So, we bit the bullet and naturally didn't buy until we got a great deal, though this meant we had to spend a lot of time renovating it, which ended up being a labor of love and a fun distraction. We then got a sign for it that said "CERTIFIKID AT THE BEACH." When Jamie and I go down, we walk the beach and boardwalk; go on runs; go in the ocean or play sports with our kids; eat crabs, ice cream, and other favorite foods; or host family and friends. We are in our happy place. Though if you have any doubt, 90 percent of our discussions are about the business so it truly is CertifiKID at the beach!

Remember, we have always mainly just reinvested the business's profits back into the business and have been fortunate to not need these funds for our lifestyle because of my law practice. So, this was the first time Jamie allowed herself to get a true reward from all her success—like that one treat she let herself have after all the blood, sweat, and tears. And she felt pride and joy to let her father (who has worked equally hard over the years FOR FREE as our CFO) and her mother (who has loaned him to us for this time) use it whenever they want, so it's their happy place as well and they too can share in this reward which they richly deserve.

WE SAY: It takes only one person to get a deal (or make a sale), and that one event can change your numbers, which can then change the mentality of the team and the entire trajectory for the business.

There were times over the course of the business where we would start to feel lethargic, bored, or frustrated, as if we were losing steam. However, every single time this happened, something new would occur to turn things around. We don't think it was luck. We think we have always pushed ourselves and others on the team to constantly stay on the move, look around the next corner, and never be satisfied or complacent. You and your team make your own luck. It takes only one new sale, or idea, or success, to turn things around and in a positive direction. If you preach this approach, and live it, you will realize it.

· 7 ·

YEAR 7
The Disaster Area

SHE SAID: When shit goes wrong (and it will), see the teaching moment instead of just the disappointment.

It was spring break, and we were taking our first big family trip! We had splurged and were headed to a gorgeous resort in Mexico that, most importantly, had a kids' club so we could finally have some time together to relax. We had decided not to travel much with the kids up until this point because we just did not think they would appreciate it and it would be a ton of work on our end. Brian also is a very stressed traveler as you'll learn later, even though he does it so much, so I'm not sure he would've survived a flight with two screaming babies.

We were excited, to say the least, for this first vacation. We arrived at the hotel and were greeted by warm smiles, cold towels, and fruity cocktails and, once settled and sunscreened, we headed off to the infinity pool. We let the kids play in the shallow area of the pool as I sipped my drink and checked my phone. My team knew we were on vacation but, as always, I would be working when the kids took naps and at night when we were in the room.

> Over the decade, I have never actually taken more than a weekend off (I'm not even sure I can think of a weekend but assume I had to have taken one). I dream of the day when I can just go completely off the grid for a week. I know it would be good for me, but we just have never had that luxury. When you're an entrepreneur or own a business, it truly is 24/7 and you must be available. This story will illustrate why.

73

Just as I lay down on my chair at the pool and looked at my phone, I was caught off guard when I saw "EMERGENCY" in the subject line of an email from our CTO, Bien. He's not the type to overreact, so this jolted me. He apologized for bothering us on vacation, but he needed to speak to us immediately. I told Brian what was going on and we scooped the kids up and told them we were going to have to go check them into the kids' club for an hour. Ugh! Seriously, this had to happen the day we arrive?

We called Bien from a bench near the pool, and he informed us that we had had a data breach. I had NO idea what in the world that meant, or what we should do about it, despite my background in security. (I'll leave it to Brian to explain the details and actions we took to address it.) As a result, the rest of our very expensive vacation was spent on our laptops or on the phone with Bien and our lawyers, insurers, and data breach consultants.

Somehow our kids still had an amazing time and to this day, reminisce about how great a trip it was, and don't even remember that we were preoccupied with this business disaster. But it was certainly not the relaxing vacation Brian and I had been dreaming about. It was super stressful and scary.

We did begin traveling more with our kids after that year and have certainly had more fun and enjoyable experiences, which were uninterrupted by the business. However, we have learned as entrepreneurs and business owners, you need to assume you will always be working and you never know when incidents will occur. In our experience, shit happens typically at the worst times (like when you're on vacation!), so prepare for the worst.

The data breach was probably the biggest incident we've had happen to us so far (knock on wood), given that we are a Web-based business, but there were always fires—big and small—around every corner. We work with thousands of businesses and thousands of customers, so we are constantly waiting for the next shoe to drop. Every morning, I'd wake up and hold my breath as there always seemed to be some issue with an unhappy business, customer, or employee. It was exhausting then and still is now.

One of the disasters that occurred very early on in the business helped us navigate and avoid many future customer service nightmares and potential crises. It happened in advance of our first Easter when we were approached by a woman who wanted to sell an Easter cake pop gift. She was based in Atlanta, very nice and easy to work with, her cake pops looked amazing, and the price point for the cake pops was reasonable, which made for a great and affordable gift. Score.

We launched the deal, and it did very well, with us selling 500 of them. I was following all the daily deal sites and noticed soon after we launched our deal that several other sites were also selling her cake pops. Hmmm. This was concerning to me because I wondered how she would be able to make and ship all those cake pops as essentially a one-woman operation. I touched base with her before Easter, and she assured me she was all good and everything was under control.

Once again, we were in our minivan heading up to Pittsburgh for the holiday (because you know now, this is when shit happens) and I saw a customer service inquiry come through about how the customer's cake pop order had not been received yet. I forwarded this along to the owner to check in and inquire about this order. No response.

The next morning, I woke up to several more angry emails from customers about their missing cake pops. I emailed the owner again with the details from the customers. Silence. A couple of hours later, I tried calling her. The call didn't go through, and the operator said the phone was disconnected. That was when I started to panic. We were three days away from Easter and I was not sure what to do.

I started Googling and grew even more concerned. She was listed on every single deal site imaginable. I even tried to contact some of the other deal sites to see if they could give me any information, but trying to get on the phone with an actual human being was a joke. I then started trying to find a relative or someone related to this cake pop owner to see if they could get in touch with her. I ended up finding and calling her aunt who hung up on me after I started explaining the situation.

While Brian and I were visiting with family and taking care of the kids, we were also trying to figure out what we were going to do about this fiasco, as it seemed like every ten minutes, I was getting pinged with a customer service email about these damn cake pops. We decided that if we didn't hear anything from the owner by morning, we would send an email out to all the customers, fall on our sword, and give them enough time to possibly get a replacement gift.

That afternoon, we received a very short and shady email from the owner suggesting that some cake pops had been shipped and others had not, but she was working on it and planned to fulfill as many of the orders as she could. She was just too overwhelmed. No apology.

We had already paid her the money from the orders, which at the time was how we and many of these daily deal sites operated. It was a big benefit for businesses to get their money up front to help with cash flow. And then a portion of purchasers would end up not redeeming their vouchers, resulting in a windfall for the business.

But this also led to many deal sites going under because businesses would run deals constantly just to get the up-front money, and if something went wrong (which it inevitably did when you're selling thousands of vouchers every day) and you had to refund customers, you'd already be out the money to the business (who wouldn't or couldn't pay you back). This cake pop incident was a key turning point that crystallized this risk to us and prompted us to change our approach.

Here is the email we ended up sending to our customers (without the name of the business):

Dear CertifiKID Purchaser,

We understand that some of you purchased the cake pop deal from [BUSINESS] and were expecting delivery by Easter. We have been in touch with the business throughout this week and were told that all the Easter deliveries were shipped, purchasers should have received UPS shipment notices, and the cake pops would be delivered between this past Thursday and today.

Despite these representations and even if you received a UPS shipment notice, we understand that some of you did not receive your cake pops by today—the day before Easter Sunday. We also understand that some of you have tried to directly contact [BUSINESS] about your orders without success.

Needless to say, we feel terrible about this. With this purchase, you have taken the time to do something thoughtful for your family or friends and were expecting these cake pops to arrive for the Easter holiday and they have not. We sincerely apologize for this unacceptable situation and, while we cannot erase the disappointment and frustration you feel, we are committed to correcting it. If your cake pops were not delivered by Easter as ordered and expected, please email us at info@certifikid.com and we will promptly refund you for the value of your purchase.

We have been featuring offers for hundreds of businesses over the past years and have never had a circumstance like this one. We pride ourselves on featuring and working with reliable businesses and promise to do our best in the future to ensure that a similar situation does not arise and our subscribers—like you—have a positive CertifiKID experience.

Please accept our apologies and we wish you and your family a happy Easter.

Best regards,
Jamie Ratner
CEO & Founder

To this day, we have never received more positive feedback from our subscribers on how we handled an issue with a deal purchase than we did with this email. It had a huge impact in helping us gain customer loyalty. I have met customers over the years who have referred to this specific incident and our handling of it as a key reason for their support and loyalty over all these years. They felt strongly that we did the right thing.

One of the keys to customer service I have learned is that you must put yourself in the customer's shoes and think how you would like an incident to be handled. Did this incident ruin my family time? Yes. Did the refunds cost us a small fortune? Yes. But was it the right thing to do and the way we would have wanted to be treated in a similar situation? Yes.

I think the fact that I too am a mom who wants a good deal, and thus in the same demographic as my subscribers, means that I can relate to and serve my subscribers in a way that other businesses can't, which has been a special secret sauce ingredient for us.

I could write an entire book just about customer stories. Our director of customer experience, Randi, and I joke about it constantly—from the mom who asked for a refund because her child did not come home from day camp with matching socks to our good friend's father who couldn't figure out how to buy a deal for his grandkids and sent a nasty expletive-filled message to our customer service email.

However, there have also been customer stories that have warmed our hearts and given us the drive to keep going, like the mom who wrote in explaining how thankful she was for a county fair deal. She said that for years she had had to take a different route whenever the fair came to town, so her son did not see it because she didn't have the money to take him. When she saw the CertifiKID deal, it was the first time she could drive by and finally take her son. He had the best time, and she was deeply appreciative.

As a business owner, particularly of an e-commerce or Web-based business, you have to thicken your skin to deal with all kinds of customers and issues. When a customer can hide behind a computer screen, it makes it very easy for them to play the role of a mean person. The best thing you can do is have someone pick up the phone and call the customer. Nine out of ten times this defuses the situation and may even earn you a more loyal customer in the process.

HE SAID: It's sad to say but, in business, some people will try to screw you, so be on guard and prepare for the worst.

Since the inception of our business, I have traveled all over the world for my law practice and have had to manage meeting my CertifiKID obligations during these travels. This often required me to fight through the exhaustion to manage small and big fires once I get back to my hotel after a late business dinner or conducting conference calls in the middle of the night. Instead of getting much-needed sleep on overnight or long flights, I'm working away on Jamie's checklist. The nature of this work has changed over time.

For example, I used to edit every single deal before it went live and wouldn't even delegate this responsibility if I were heading to China for a week. Once we put our core team in place and were doing much bigger business, the work became more high level but also more complex, stressful, and in need of careful attention, such as finance, partnership, legal, or HR issues.

For someone who travels as much as I do, I really don't like it. I'm a walking stress case. Even if I am in business class, I'm stressing about overhead luggage space or getting on and off the plane first. I move through airports like a bank robber trying to get in and out as quickly as possible without leaving a trace. I am not the person who wants to sit next to someone who is chatty and really enjoying the fun and adventure of travel. When others hear about where I have been or where I am going, they think it is cool and are envious. But I no longer see or feel the appeal of it. It's just part of the drill.

For Jamie, too, I think there was a period where I was like a blur to her—sometimes there, other times not; usually accessible, but rarely engaged enough. I plan my business trips so I am on the ground for the absolute least amount of time possible. Many of my colleagues and friends never understood this. Why not spend the extra day or weekend in Beijing, Tokyo, Rio, Seoul, Amsterdam, or Paris? But I never needed the extra sightseeing time, or meal, or culture. I wanted to be there for my family.

Of course, Jamie thought this was pointless because I would race home after a long and exhausting trip but be so out of it mentally and physically that I was of no use to her or the kids. She'd joke (but not really) that on arrival I should stay at the airport hotel for the night so she could avoid the pain and suffering of dealing with me when I got home. From my perspective, I'd step one foot in the house and be greeted with no "welcome home" balloon, kiss, affection, or space. Instead, I'd be showered with all the things we (and I) needed to do the next day or over the weekend. It would go in one ear and out the other, which would lead her to say she was just going to avoid talking to me for 24 hours until I was able to hold a conversation. Hmph.

I think this reflected a bit of resentment as I was able to get away from the family and business and at least get some time to myself, which she never has been able to do. It also reflected the pressure of the growth and success of the business falling mainly on her shoulders. Even with our strong management team and numbers, she always felt mired in personnel or administrative issues and thus struggled to be creative and act like an entrepreneur, which as you now know was her true passion.

At various times before kids, Jamie would come on business trips with me, and we would often extend them into a vacation. We went to amazing places like Australia, Tokyo, Beijing, London, Spain, and Greece. I'd work during the day and she'd run around the cities by herself, which she loved. But once we had kids and started the business, joining me on trips was not an option until much later when the kids went to sleepaway camp.

Our Cancun vacation and data breach event are a good example. We were thinking we would try to limit screen time at the resort but instead were greeted with the data breach news literally upon our arrival. I immediately shifted into legal and crisis management mode.

Once we spoke to our CTO Bien and got the details of what happened, I called my buddy Doug, our legal counsel. He got his data breach team on the line, and we discussed options for addressing the issue internally, and what our obligations were in terms of external notification. We then got on the phone with our insurer, explained the situation, and put them on notice about the event. In about 24 hours, we talked to all our advisors, got recommendations, decided on the strategy, and began implementation.

Our financial exposure was potentially very substantial—in the hundreds of thousands of dollars or more—and the legal and expert costs of implementing our plan would cost hundreds of thousands of dollars, which fortunately would all be covered by our insurance. In the end, we were able to manage the event prudently and efficiently while ensuring that our subscribers continued to have confidence using our platform. In other words, the event did not lead to a business disruption or loss of subscribers. But it was scary.

During the same period, we had an issue with a science camp for which we sold hundreds of vouchers for their locations all over the country. They insisted on getting paid their share of the voucher purchases (i.e., 70 percent of the revenue) thirty days BEFORE the camp sessions were held since most of their costs were incurred before the camps started. We reluctantly agreed and quickly regretted the decision.

As the camp sessions started, complaints began rolling in from parents about how they had taken their kids to camp only to be turned away and told the session was canceled because not enough kids had enrolled. Others had been able to go to camp for a day or two and then the rest of the week was canceled for random reasons.

We frantically called the owners—a young couple—and simply encouraged them to refund everyone and come clean with us about what they could do and couldn't do to stop the bleeding. But their response was that all the money had already been spent, they had overextended themselves, felt awful, and would do right by us and the customers. We pushed and pushed, and threatened them about their breach of our contract, but were lucky to get a call back.

Of course, this left us in the position of dealing with our customers. Just as we did with the cake pops, we made the decision to provide refunds to anyone who needed one or asked for one and to seek reimbursement from the owners. When we finally got a response, they said they were broke and filing for bankruptcy. They promised to pay us back at some point. This was my cue to begin the process of getting our insurance to cover this loss, which was more than $10,000.

For Jamie, it was personal. She hates feeling duped more than anything, so she drew on her security background and went into detective mode. She scoured the internet and discovered on their social media pages that while we were paying these refunds, the owners had a fancy wedding, went on a Caribbean honeymoon, and bought a new house! Not a good look.

We did get an insurance payout, and I'm sure you'll be surprised to hear that we haven't gotten a dime from the owners, and they even started another science camp under a different name once they came out of bankruptcy. Jamie pokes them every year about their debt just to show them that she will NOT forget.

In addition to increasing our insurance, we learned from this episode that we should never pay a camp before their session is held unless we have complete trust in the camp. And we never did. If it costs us business, so be it. It is not worth the risk.

Through these experiences and many others, what I have learned in business time and again is that you can't think like a lawyer. There are issues where someone explains to you what is legally permissible, advisable, or where there are grey areas. And internally, I often play this role. You absorb all this guidance and then must decide what is the right thing to do from the business perspective, which doesn't always align. Is an approach necessary or simply preferred? What is the risk there will be an issue or problem if we take this or that course? What is your comfort level with taking this risk?

For example, early on, Groupon and many of their competitors would limit or even hide their deal terms in the offers that were emailed to their subscribers. Their goal with a 24-hour deal was to make every day feel like Black Friday. If people didn't act fast, they would lose out on the deal. This dynamic led people to not read the fine print prior to purchasing. Of course, once they read the deal terms, which often would be when they were on their way to the event or restaurant, they'd realize there were limitations to the deal, such as "weekday only" or "one voucher per household." This led to an enormous amount of customer complaints and refund issues.

But it was a volume game for Groupon and they didn't really care about customer service. You seriously could never get someone on the phone if you had any issue—trust us, we tried regarding Groupons that we ourselves bought! With 20 million subscribers, how much time will they devote to any one subscriber's issue?

Meanwhile, we approached this dynamic by differentiating ourselves from our behemoth competitors through favorable, consumer-friendly, and transparent terms and conditions. We spelled out all the deal restrictions and conditions in extensive detail at the end of every deal in real, normal-sized text, not fine print. We also ensured they were legally and commercially sound. Everyone on the team complained to me that our deal write-ups were too long, difficult to read on a smartphone, hard to understand, not all necessary, and therefore costing us sales and money. But Jamie and I didn't care and wanted to be conservative with our approach to these risks.

As a result, we seriously limited any refund and customer service issues in the early period that other sites were struggling with, which ensured these issues did not weigh down our leanly staffed operation. This resulted in a high level of customer and member satisfaction and loyalty which, as discussed previously, is a source of pride for us. In essence, this was a trade-off between risk and reward that we were happy to make.

WE SAY: As soon as you make money, get insurance because disaster will strike, usually while you're on vacation, so protect yourself so you can take more calculated risks.

Once you are doing big enough business, confronting actual risks, or anticipating potential risks, it's time to ensure you have sufficient insurance in place for all aspects of your business. And then over-insure by topping up what is the minimum you are advised to put in place.

After more than ten years in business, we believe the most successful people are those who (1) make the quickest decisions and then implement those decisions quickly, and (2) take the most *measured* risks. The third key ingredient is luck.

As you now know, one of us (Jamie) is conservative and not a big risk taker. And the other one (Brian) is not a quick decision-maker. So how did we succeed where others have failed? We think the answer is that we balanced each other concerning (1) and (2) and then made our own luck. Find that balance.

· 8 ·

YEAR 8

The Plateau

**SHE SAID: When you are negative, frustrated, and dissatisfied
(like I was at this time), stop faking it and tell your
team how you feel and why. They can handle it.**

Once we got past the data breach, it was smooth sailing. I had my team in place, we were seeing solid sales, drama was low, and all seemed rosy. My kids were now ten and nine, so more independent, which was life-changing. This is probably the point in the story where you'd think I was sitting back with a glass of wine and kicking my feet up to enjoy the fruits of our labor. Nope! Year eight is what I have deemed "the year of the bitch."

Yes, we were making a lot of money, but I was frustrated because I feared the business was plateauing. As a result, I was constantly pissed off at many on the sales team, who I often imagined sitting back with *their* glasses of wine, kicking their feet up, and collecting money, and not working. Fairly or not my impression was they were just rerunning the same old low-hanging fruit deals and not putting the time in to get new and exciting ones. This mood was evident to the team when I shot off sharp emails at the end of each week which reeked of my unhappiness. Let's just say I have never been good at hiding my feelings!

Brian and I racked our brains 24/7 about ways to grow our subscriber base more nationally so we could sell more deals in more places but realized none of the ideas were ever going to get us a million new subscribers. We tried out many ideas that year with the hope that something would go viral! But there was no silver bullet. We were finally at a point where we would have invested significantly in something that we really thought might take off. Up until then, I had been extremely conservative on the advertising and marketing side of the business, but I was ready now to do some testing and pay the price.

One of the most exciting opportunities we explored was meeting with the head of partnerships at the *Washington Post* (yes, my boyfriend reporter Tom's paper). It turned out that he had gone to my high school and was a big CertifiKID subscriber. We had an incredible two-hour meeting with his team and decided to move forward with a partnership—the *Post* would give us a giant spread each week where we would feature a super-exciting deal with a special discount code for *Post* readers so we could track sales through the ad.

We spent hours crafting the perfect ad and used the opportunity as an enticement to get big local businesses to run deals with us. Everyone on the team thought this was the opportunity of a lifetime, considering the trade value for an ad this size in a major newspaper was equal to a year's salary for some people!

But we featured four different deals over four weeks and saw very limited sales or sign-ups. I was crushed. Doesn't anyone read the newspaper anymore? How is this even possible? UGH!

This was just one of the many growth concepts we tested. In the end, we always saw our biggest bump in subscriber numbers when we featured something exciting, especially a new concept or venue. I pushed the team hard to focus on these types of businesses, which worked to a degree, but the reality was that it was not enough to significantly change the trajectory of our business. There was no silver bullet to achieve the mass scaling we thought was possible.

Aside from trying to grow our subscriber base, I was always looking for avenues to help expand the business in other ways. As mentioned, I tried hard to make the deals unique and exciting to keep the customers engaged, which I believe is part of CertifiKID's secret sauce. Here are examples of some of the most unique deals we ran over the years: kangaroo farm experience; ice cream tour with a local dairy farm; tiny house getaway; and s'more family staycation experience at a local hotel. These were all experiences you could not get elsewhere that generated big buzz and led to people sharing the deals, which spread them like wildfire!

We also did programs to engage with the local PTAs, launched a camp scholarship program, invested in an influencer campaign, and opened a deal segment for families of children with special needs. The list goes on and on. I never sit still and am never complacent. I always look for a new angle around every corner.

Along with my frustration over the business's growth, I think one of the other things that led to my bitchiness with my team was boredom (which is also why I was trying other concepts constantly). We were running the same deals season after season like clockwork. How much longer were we going to keep doing this even though it was more than paying the bills?

They say that when a business stops growing, it dies. Thus, it was time to start thinking about new business ideas. Should I start something new in parallel with CertifiKID? Once again, this led me to spout out idea after idea to Brian like I did pre-CertifiKID. Was I just doing this to distract myself from my inability to get CertifiKID to the next level?

Upon reflection, I think the person I was really mad at was myself. How could I not figure out how to get this business to explode? We had all the ingredients, and the deal space was more open than ever before. All we needed was some gasoline to put on the fire. But what was that missing puzzle piece we needed? I was obsessed with finding it and had spent eight years trying, but it was still unclear to me what our next move should be. I spent every waking minute and probably most of my dreams trying to solve this. Solve us. Solve me.

Meanwhile, Brian was obsessed with the concept that we needed to be at $10 million in annual revenue by our tenth year: "10 in 10" he would chant at our team meetings. It had a nice ring to it. We hit $6 million in top line sales this year which was only about 5 percent growth over the prior year. How would we get to $10 million in two years when it felt like we were plateauing? I started to have doubts and expressed to Brian that maybe I was not the right person to be the CEO anymore to get us there.

However, deep down I knew there was no one who would give this business the 200 percent I was giving it mentally, but I also knew I had zero experience scaling a business other than my own. I understood my limitations. I was an entrepreneur at heart—or a MomPreneur/ParentPreneur—not a "CEO" in the traditional sense or even an experienced business leader. I wondered if a fancy Harvard MBA-type was the missing piece.

I never expressed any of this doubt to my team. As a leader, you fear showing your team any weakness or lacking the answers to the business's core challenges. On the other hand, having this mindset of fear and then taking it out on everyone else was clearly not the best strategy either. If I had been more open and honest with everyone, maybe it would have taken the stress off my shoulders and spread some shared responsibility across the team.

My frustration spilled into other aspects of our lives. I found myself being less patient with my kids. I had always been a quiet and calm mom, but my volume had gone up in the house. I was also snapping at Brian left and right. I never used to curse, but it now felt like I was doing it every other word. It was clear I was not at my best!

Because I have been guilty of doing this myself, I have learned to have more patience when someone around me is uncharacteristically acting like an asshole. I try to check myself before overreacting and remember I might not know what else is going on in their life that caused their change in behavior.

I needed to do something . . . and fast!

I looked inward to change my spirits and bring myself some much-needed perspective. This is when an opportunity presented itself to express my appreciation for my dad, Gary (or "Daddy" as I always called him), our CFO. Brian was always horrified when I called him "Daddy" in our team meetings. I didn't care and would always make this (not so) innocent mistake just to see Brian's reaction!

I nominated my dad for the *Washington Business Journal*'s CFO of the Year Award, and he was one of the twenty winners! It was wonderful to see my dad receive an award like this which was well deserved.

My dad took on the role of helping us with our books back when we started the business in 2010. He has carried this task as our CFO every day since and helped guide us financially as we have grown. He retired early from the IRS after a thirty-year stint. He started at twenty-five and planned his career meticulously so he could retire young at fifty-five. He never imagined he'd be killing himself for ten years as our CFO after offering to help us when he was sixty-five. Brian always jokes that Gary has never worked harder in his life, which is true.

He was the dad whose primary focus was on his family and his kids, not his career. He was home every day for dinner and attended every soccer game and school event. His work was never an excuse for anything in our home. I realize now how lucky I am to have a dad like this and often question if Brian and I veer too far from this important example.

The opportunity to work with my dad on this business for years, and for it to be such a fun and rewarding second career for him, is truly one of the greatest gifts the business has given me. Though I know it has taken him away from my mom and the poker table (he probably could be professional if he had the time!), I feel his engagement with young people on our team and the complexities and challenge of his work has been great for his mental and physical health. I hope he agrees!

Brian and I feel fortunate for all his tireless (and often thankless) work and support. He treats every penny like it is important, which allows us to be smartly managed and have complete trust in the business's finances.

This accolade and focus on my daddy were the jolt I needed during this time to keep myself going and cast aside any doubt that I was the right leader for my business. It was also a nice distraction from me turning the "big 4-0" and the passing of Brian's dad, Jimmy.

HE SAID: When faced with personal adversity or grief, work can be the best medicine.

During the summer of this year, my parents did the unthinkable. They sold their home outside Pittsburgh and moved to Maryland, twenty minutes from our home. I had been pushing my parents to downsize and move to be near us since my sister also now lived in Washington, DC, after a twenty-year stint in San Francisco. So, their two kids and only two grandkids all lived in the same area. At a certain point, I realized that my pushing was having the opposite effect, so I stopped. And they came to the decision on their own. This is a good tip!

The reason I never thought my folks would move is that they lived in the town where my dad had deep roots. Three generations of his family lived there and built the family car business. As I mentioned earlier, when my dad sold the business, my dream of running it would never be realized and I knew I'd have to chart my own path.

This is one of those life events that is out of your control and profoundly impacts your destiny. I feel I was lucky that things turned out this way for me. But I also think my dad was very unlucky that things turned out the way they did for him. If his dad had lived longer, he could have studied under his tutelage and maybe instead of selling at the first opportunity, he would have hung in there and expanded like many other local dealers ended up doing.

I remember driving down a stretch of highway in my hometown and seeing someone else's name on car dealerships and thinking that could be our name. We would always talk about the importance of the timing of business decisions, reflecting on his own experience with a level of nostalgia. When do you scale up, scale down, or maintain? When do you take risks and go for it and how do you protect yourself, so any falls aren't so steep?

When we started CertifiKID, my dad loved it and found his kindred spirit in Jamie. He would ask about the business and how it was doing and the two of them would talk shop. He was in awe of her entrepreneurship and ability to get things done. He could truly relate to what we were doing, our successes and struggles, and was proud of her and what we were doing together. He also always told us that his biggest regrets in business related to not taking more risks.

My dad had been struggling with MDS (myelodysplastic syndrome), a pre-leukemic condition and a form of blood cancer, for almost twenty years. When he was diagnosed, a doctor said the odds were that he had five to eight years to live. He outlived that projection by ten years and let that doctor know it when he randomly ran into him during one of his many hospital stints. I smile when I picture how that conversation went and my dad's satisfaction in that moment. The doctor was gracious and said—"good for you."

The disease took its toll on him over time but in the last three to four years it was especially taxing. He had a very weak immune system from the drugs he was on so he would get sick easily and had several bouts of pneumonia that would put him in the hospital for two to four weeks at a time, and then it would take him a few months to recover when he got home. And then this cycle would repeat itself.

After a recent bout over the Christmas holiday during this year, we weren't surprised when the doctor said we should consider hospice, though my dad was surprised. Because he was always fighting to get better, I don't think he let himself come to terms with the reality that it was a losing battle. This felt like he was being advised to give up even though he had more fight in him.

He came to terms with this plan and, like a lot of patients who enter hospice, because of the change in approach to his medication, he had a big rebound when he got home. He had more energy and was able to go out to dinner and do things with my mom and our family.

He always wanted to go to the new National Air and Space Museum after moving to the DC area, but we hadn't been able to make it there due to his health. One day, he said he was up for it, and my son and I took him in his wheelchair. He was a plane and war buff, so knew the names of everything on display in the museum. We had a great time and it proved to be one of his last outings as he soon took a fall at home, which led to a downward spiral. He passed away in early March.

I lost my best friend. The friend concept hadn't really crystallized in my mind until he passed as I started to think of all that we did together—literally hand in hand. And he was a great dad too. Support, encouragement, trust, honesty, pride, advice, warmth, a keen interest in what I was doing, a leader by example—all great ingredients and ones I try to model with my own kids and with my work.

When you lose someone of great significance in your life and have other responsibilities, how do you react? It took about a year for it to really hit me and, naturally, a lot of extra support was required for my mom who was now all alone in a new town for the first time in fifty years. Thankfully, my sister was able to give my mom so much of the emotional support and time that I struggled to provide, given all that we had on our plate. My mom is a true extrovert—she is where I get it from—and somehow she was able to muster the strength to build such a true blessing.

My way of dealing with the grief and the hole in my heart was to work. It was good medicine. And I did so with my dad's words of wisdom in the back of my mind about regretting not taking more risks.

Therefore, when we had an opening to meet with LivingSocial's new CEO in their posh DC offices, Jamie and I jumped at the chance. As I mentioned earlier, LivingSocial was cofounded by the *Washington Post*'s former publisher's son-in-law. Amazon was a huge early investor and they set themselves up as Groupon's primary competitor. They had an enormous email list, amazing connections, and generated hundreds of millions in revenue. They soon became DC's largest private employer and decked out the Old Post Office Building in the heart of DC.

However, like Groupon, they were never profitable and on the back of Groupon's underwhelming IPO (initial public offering), their IPO strategy changed, and they kept pivoting. One day it was restaurant deals and delivery. The next day they were all about experiences and pushing their family edition in direct competition with us. The next day it was products. You get the gist. They sold their Korean outfit for $230 million to Groupon which helped keep them afloat for a while, but soon their management team resigned, and they brought in a new ex-Google executive as their CEO.

Jamie friended him on LinkedIn, asked for a meeting, and the next thing you know we were walking into the Old Post Office Building. Jamie's thought was that they should let us be their "family edition."

Jamie is fearless with blind outreach like this, which is a key ingredient to her success. She has no fear or shame in reaching out to anyone, regardless of their position or status. She always says, "What is the worst that can happen? They ignore me or say 'no.'"

As we walked into their amazing space, we were struck by all the empty offices and cubicles. It had a "dead man walking" feeling. We were soon escorted to a swanky conference room as the CEO and a few of his colleagues sat down to join us for the meeting. In my other world, I would never go into a meeting like this without being overprepared. I'd have a slide deck ready to explain CertifiKID and our vision, why we had asked for the meeting, and what we wanted from LivingSocial.

But here is where reality set in. We had been SO busy between the kids and the business, we didn't have much time, so we ended up preparing on the drive downtown. This is typically the way Jamie rolls. Fast and furious, no BS, and no waste of time. Her view is other CEOs don't need this kind of fluff and are happy to cut to the chase. It has worked well for her, but often puts me in some uncomfortable situations, like this one, where she expects me to take the lead.

Therefore, without the glossy backdrop of a slide deck, we introduced ourselves and explained what we saw as an opportunity for a partnership. It helped that they knew who we were, given we both had the same home base of Washington, DC, and they said some nice things about our business and what we had built. The CEO then cut to the chase and revealed that they were involved in an internal audit to focus the business on their core strengths, which were restaurants and experiences. They were therefore not going to focus on niche areas like their family edition.

When we suggested that we could run this edition for them, they said they were open to partnering in some way at some point on the family business, but not at that time, given their very targeted agenda. In other words, by reducing their headcount, overall expenses, and focusing resources only in their major revenue-generating areas, their primary objective was to get more balance with their P&L (profit and loss).

After a pleasant, hour-long meeting, Jamie and I left the building, got in our minivan for the short ride home, and said to each other that the CEO's mood music sounded eerily familiar to what my high school friend (also an ex-Google executive) was saying when she was brought in as CEO to help get Plum District in the position to sell.

This proved prophetic. Within a year, LivingSocial sold to Groupon for zero cash. They were never again a competitor of ours in the family space and this left Groupon as really the only site doing overlapping deals with us. Of course, we didn't really consider Groupon a competitor because they were a billion-dollar public company, and we liked the fact that we could watch them and what they were doing as a market leader investing in our space. We could choose to follow certain trends or adjust them to fit within our niche platform.

But because there was now this larger national opening in the deal space, we would go into the next year feeling even more pressure to do something bold to finally help scale our business nationally. The time was now for us to go for it.

WE SAY: When you plateau (and you will), look in the mirror, make no excuses, work harder, and have no fear of mixing things up.

When you feel you've hit a brick wall and can't break through, even though you feel like you've tried everything, it can be paralyzing. You fear taking risks because you're pessimistic about the result. The more fatalistic and desperate you become, the more you struggle.

Meanwhile, once you have any kind of success, it can have a domino effect: things come more easily and you feel unstoppable. You can't be complacent. You can't take your foot off the gas. Keep knocking on the door, taking risks, and trying to mix it up. Understand that it's a journey and that you have to go through the valleys to get to the top of the mountain.

· 9 ·

YEAR 9

Swimming with the Sharks

**SHE SAID: Don't wait, don't overthink,
don't second-guess. Just make your own luck.**

I was scrolling through Groupon, seeing what they were featuring that day, when my phone rang. It was my mom. "Hi Sweetie! I was watching the news and saw *Shark Tank* is coming this week to the Verizon Center in DC to do auditions. Thought you might be interested."

Without taking a breath, she moved on to talking about her latest shopping trip to Sam's Club and all her finds as I pretended to listen while Googling to learn more about the audition. The show would be coming in just a few days and the audition would consist of doing a pitch to their casting producers, just like you would do to the Sharks. I thanked my mom (cutting her short) and immediately texted Brian the link.

BRIAN: No chance. I am not waiting in that line all day.

ME: PLEASE!

BRIAN: We don't have the time to get ready for this.

ME: I'll do everything. It's just one metro stop for you.

BRIAN: Yeah right.

ME: PLEASE. It's our chance.

BRIAN: I'm not sure. Let's take the day to think about it.

I then remembered that a *Shark Tank* casting director had reached out to me in 2011, but we (Brian) felt it was too soon. I looked him up and discovered he no longer worked on the show, but I used his email to find another casting director on LinkedIn and took an educated guess on his email based on my original contact's old email. I sent an email to this address, asking if I could discuss getting on the show. Less than 24 hours later, I got a response that the casting director wanted to have a call with me. Boom.

Before I knew it, I had bypassed the all-day in-person casting call at Verizon Center and had advanced to the next round. Whoo-hoo! My euphoria lasted until I shared with Brian what Round 2 looked like. There were about 100 pages of forms to complete, and we needed to create a two-minute video. And it was all due in two weeks. And this was in June when we were intensely busy with the kids finishing their school year, taking a short vacation, and then getting the kids off to their summer sleepaway camp.

Why would we go through this and put ourselves out there in this way, especially when the business was doing well? It was not for the money, which is typically the reason businesses go on *Shark Tank* (i.e., for the funding).

But I had always wondered what national exposure like going on *Shark Tank* could provide us. I also wondered what we could accomplish if we had a strategic partner who had experience guiding businesses like ours to the next level and, specifically, could help us replicate our strengths in new markets and scale our business nationally. Looking back, I don't think I had a clue what I was signing up for but just loved the idea of focusing on something new and exciting for a few minutes.

In my mind it was not even a question if we should keep going with the application process. And if we needed to skip some questions because we didn't have the time or information to answer them and do an amateurish video, that would still be worthwhile. What did we have to lose? Brian would have nothing of it. He was back and forth on whether we should go down this road and kept telling me if we were going to do this, we had to do it the right way and go for it hard because we'd likely only have one shot.

My job was taking care of the video and he took care of the reams of paperwork. I found a local guy on Upwork to help us put together a video. We took a bunch of videos on our iPhones and then emailed them to him to put together with some graphics and make it look cool and professional.

Brian and my dad worked day and night on the paperwork, huffing and puffing their way through it. I think it was more time consuming for us because we were more established than businesses that typically go on *Shark Tank*. We had almost ten years of history to report on, including extensive financial information. We killed ourselves for two weeks, even getting our kids involved in the video, wrapped it all up in a nice bow, and sent it off to the producers feeling like we gave it our best shot.

About two weeks later, we got an email congratulating us on making it to the next phase and assigning us two producers to guide us going forward. No freakin' way! We got on a call with our two producers, who were both young and enthusiastic, though they did pour some cold water on our excitement. The first thing they told us was that we couldn't tell a soul we were even talking to them, and the process was highly confidential. They reiterated over and over that no one could know we were in this process with the show or at this stage and if anyone found out, we would lose our opportunity and be cut.

The other big point they made clear was that there would be weekly eliminations of applicants. It was late June, and we would speak to them weekly over the next two months creating our potential pitch, while the executive producers continued to analyze our application. Our producers would report to their bosses how our pitch was developing (and how we were doing), which would be a big factor in whether we would make it to the following week.

Our producers were very creative and fun guys, and I genuinely think they liked us and wanted us to make it on the show. In the end, I believe the key reason we made it through to the filming stage was my costume idea. We had gone through lots of concepts for how we could visualize our family-focused deal site on TV, but it all seemed too cheesy, just focused on a video and picture scroll, or it didn't capture the essence of the business.

But then I stumbled upon this rollercoaster costume that a family could wear and pretend they were at an amusement park, bringing to life our business being about family experiences outside the home. Our twenty-something producers were over the moon with excitement about it.

Our kids went off to camp and we spent the next seven weeks working on our potential pitch and honing our script. Even though our producers seemed to express more confidence in us every week, we knew they were not the decision-makers so were always anxious about being cut or getting confirmation that we would be flying out to LA for the taping.

The kids arrived home from camp in mid-August and we took them to the beach before school started. As soon as we arrived, the call came. We had made it to the taping round and were scheduled to fly out to LA in two weeks in early September! Of course, we were reminded by our producers to stay focused because making it to the taping round and flying to LA does not guarantee you will get to do your pitch and get taped. And getting taped does not guarantee your pitch will ever air. We'll discuss this more later.

Since people always ask, to summarize, here are our primary lessons for putting yourself in the best position to get a *Shark Tank* taping:

1. **There is always a back door. Find it and use it!**
2. **You must be proactive, think creatively, and set yourself apart to get selected for a show like *Shark Tank*.**
3. **Make it EASY for your producers or handlers so they want to keep you around.**

* * * *

To say those two weeks before our taping were frenetic is an understatement. We watched every single *Shark Tank* episode we possibly could. We memorized our pitch. We ordered props for our set, which included a giant pirate ship and huge photo boards of our kids and our employees' kids engaged in experiences using our deals. We went back and forth on whether we should let our kids miss their first week of school to be a part of the experience and on the (costume) rollercoaster. They were begging to go. We ultimately decided to have my parents fly them out for the second part of the week so the four of them would be part of the rollercoaster along with our COO Amie and her daughter Macy, who were thrilled when they got the invite.

The day finally arrived, and Brian and I flew out to LA. It was exciting on many levels and special to share together. It was one of those times in your life when you don't know what to expect but know the experience will be unforgettable. We went to Santa Monica that first night where we strolled the boardwalk and then went for a run to Venice. We did some last-minute shopping to make sure we had everything perfect for our wardrobes and continued to practice our pitch everywhere we went to the point where we felt confident for our rehearsal the next day. We hit the sack early because the next day was a biggie!

The next morning, we were picked up in our hotel lobby with a dozen or so of the other entrepreneurs for a meeting and rehearsal. I really enjoyed this part. I loved meeting all the other entrepreneurs and hearing their stories and learning about their businesses. I was impressed by every person I met.

Our rehearsal was that afternoon. It was cool being at the studio and on the set. We even got our own trailer. We did our pitch for the producers; some of the producers filled in for our family as extras for the "action" part of our presentation (i.e., the rollercoaster). They had fun with it and the producers laughed like crazy. Brian and I did a good job and felt a sense of relief, given we had heard about people not making it to the taping based on their performance during rehearsals.

We were totally burned out after we finished, but decided we needed some inspiration, so we took an Uber to Inspiration Point in Hollywood for a hike. We also used the time to go through our Q&A and get prepared, quizzing each other on every possible question that the Sharks might ask and rehearsing our answers. After the hike, we had a delicious sushi dinner in Beverly Hills and passed out for the night.

The next day was a free day. My parents arrived with our kids and Amie and Macy arrived as well. We headed back to Santa Monica Pier with everyone and let the kids go on the rides. What a hooky day for them!

Brian and I stayed up late practicing as much as we could. Brian was up even later, studying our financials so he had a handle on everything that could possibly come up with the Sharks during the Q&A. He even had calls with our external lawyers and accountants to ensure we were accurate with all our planned responses.

We didn't even know until ten o'clock that night that we were confirmed for taping the next day, but thankfully our time was late morning so we could get a decent night's sleep. On taping day, we were awakened by a makeup artist and hair stylist that I'd hired to come to my hotel room to help get me ready. I felt like I was getting ready to go to a Hollywood awards show!

When we got to the set, we hit an unexpected hurdle—it turned out the kids were legally required to be tutored for three hours since it was a school day! Let's just say they were NOT happy! Because of the time required for tutoring, we were the *last* business to tape for the day.

We sat around in our trailers the entire afternoon until dark. During this down time, we ate snacks, lunched, practiced (including with the kids after their tutoring was over), studied, got some makeup and hair touch-ups, and tried to stay calm.

Finally, around 6:00 p.m., we were called to the set. At that point, things happened super-fast, and it was all surreal. I have never felt so nervous in my life (even on my wedding day!). I could not remember my pitch. I could barely talk without my teeth chattering. I remember the kids telling me I would do well, the producers telling me to breathe, and squeezing Brian's hand as hard as I could.

After an excruciating time in the Tank, my absolute favorite memory of the entire experience was coming back to our trailer on a golf cart. As we pulled into the area we had been hanging out in all day, we heard voices in the darkness on the beautiful warm evening. The kids were chanting "Who Did You Get?" and jumping up and down as we pulled up. I remember Brian announcing, "We got Mr. Wonderful!" and forming a giant group hug. Everyone was screaming with delight after a brutally long day.

We quickly got pulled away, as the protocol was for us to debrief with a psychologist. We were on a high, but I can imagine how others could be devastated after being ripped to shreds about their life's work. The psychologist explained how this would be a tough road for us to go down, especially not being able to tell anyone, and that she was there if we ever needed someone to talk to. Then Kevin O'Leary's second in command, Alan, came into the trailer to say hello, congratulate us, and tell us about next steps. I'll let Brian talk about that part.

After a sleepless night, the next morning when we flew back home, I was on an extreme a high. However, I also realized I would be living with this secret for months to come. How was I supposed to go about my life normally after an experience like this? Would our deal go through? Would our episode air, and if so, when? What did I say in the Tank and how would they make us look in the episode?

This leads me to one final lesson: **when you have a BIG experience, memorialize it all in writing the second it's over.** After a monumental event like this one, you will start to get a foggy brain and forget (or block out) what really happened. I wrote everything down on my plane ride home so I would not forget a thing—which has served me well, as I have done a good bit of writing and speaking on the *Shark Tank* experience (not to mention this chapter!).

* * * *

About six months after the show's taping, our deal with Kevin closed. It was a celebratory mood in our house.

HE SAID: If you decide to go for a game-changing opportunity, don't do it in a half-assed way; give it your all and have no regrets.

I never wanted to go on *Shark Tank*. I didn't think we needed it. I wanted us to find other, more traditional ways to scale our business, even though we had struggled to do so in the past. But Jamie was convinced of the value of going on the show and felt the time was right with the LivingSocial sale to Groupon and we had nothing to lose (other than our entire summer!). Luckily, Jamie got the show's producers to let us go straight to the application process, as she explained.

As usual, her view was to not worry about every detail and just submit "whatever." If they wanted us, the i-dotting and t-crossing wouldn't matter. As usual, I disagreed. I don't like investing time and energy into something we aren't giving our all to, once we decide it's something we should truly go for. So, I worked the team to the bone (especially my father-in-law, Gary!) in the application and preparation process. I believe it helped make the difference for us. Jamie probably disagrees.

When we finally got the call that we would be going to LA for the taping, it was a jolt of reality. This was happening for real, and I suddenly found myself wanting it. So as Jamie and I were walking all over

LA, hiking in the mountains, running on the beach, riding in Ubers, or enjoying avocado toast, we were practicing our presentation and Q&A. In other words, we were working just like we always seemed to be when traveling to fun places.

We were also fixated on what we were wearing. My specially ordered CertifiKID branded jacket was too big (I was swimming in it) and I was panicking that the new one wouldn't get delivered to the set by taping time. We were running around town looking for an alternative as our colleague Olga was feverishly trying to find something online that could get made and shipped before the taping. Ironically, the replacement jacket literally made it to the set one hour before the taping right as my bald spot was getting touched up in the makeup trailer (yes, I was told everyone on TV does it). Phew.

It was fun, but also exhausting and stressful waiting all day on the Sony set as our kids were getting their school hours in under the supervision of the show's tutor, which was quite the curveball. Finally, we were taken to the *Shark Tank* set in a golf cart, got our final touch-ups, and instructions from the producers, and there Jamie and I stood in front of the huge doors. It was show time.

Jamie was squeezing my hand hard, and I think her nervousness, which I had never seen before, ironically calmed me down and distracted me because I was worried about her.

The doors finally opened, we walked through, and stopped at our mark. We then had to stare at the Sharks in awkward silence for thirty seconds, which felt like thirty minutes. The green light flashed and Jamie started our presentation, which went off without a hitch. All the practicing paid off! And the Sharks LOVED the rollercoaster and our kids. They were laughing hysterically. It shows how creative Jamie is to come up with an idea like that.

We went into the Tank asking for $600,000 in exchange for an 8 percent stake in CertifiKID, a $7.5 million post-money valuation. This request was not pulled out of the air but followed an intense analysis and debate over several scenarios. I worked extensively on the valuation with our lawyers and accountants in advance of the taping and wanted to make sure that our request was grounded in real revenue and P&L data, historic performance, realistic future projections, and reasonable valuation metrics.

It was a difficult strategic decision because we didn't need the money and were looking for a strategic partnership. Thus, we wanted to give enough equity to make it interesting for the Sharks, but we also wanted the valuation to reflect the value of the business we had built over almost ten years and our substantial revenue numbers and profitability, which few companies have going into the Tank.

We also wanted to make the percentage low enough to give us room to offer more, if necessary, as opposed to starting higher but then having limited room to maneuver to secure a deal. While all other aspects of our presentation needed to be locked well in advance of the taping, we could choose to change our "ask" right up until the taping itself. And we in fact didn't make the final decision until literally the night before.

When Jamie said what we were asking for, Daymond said under his breath "this is uncomfortable," suggesting that it was very steep (i.e., how could we be asking for $600,000 at a $7.5 million valuation?). My job was to mainly focus on the numbers, so I knew they were going to go after me pretty quickly in the Q&A, which they did. But I was ready. We had rehearsed over and over every possible question. I teased them and then dropped the bomb that we had done *$30 million* in sales since inception and had $700,000 in net income the prior year. They were floored. Kevin said that, before hearing this, he thought we were "poo on a stick."

Three Sharks made us offers, Kevin O'Leary, Barbara Corcoran, and Daymond John. We were obviously delighted to get three offers, but disappointed that all three initial asks were for more than twice the equity we offered. We were prepared for this possibility and had gamed out all the scenarios and set limits on what we were willing to give up. However, we had not figured on Kevin including a liquidation preference in his offer, which proved to be a bit of a distraction as I discuss below!

Despite feeling we were unique for entrepreneurs who go on the show in terms of our maturity as a business, profitability, and sales/revenue numbers, we knew that the Sharks always want a premium and any real-world valuation is not typically the benchmark they use in formulating their offers and negotiating. Their thinking is that they are not regular passive investors because of the assistance they will give you in the future, the exposure you will get on their social media channels, and the show's exposure. We had more flexibility with this premium issue because we didn't have other external investors to factor in when considering the opportunity to partner with one of the Sharks.

While we were open to all the Sharks and saw the benefits that each of them could provide, Kevin O'Leary was clearly the one that we were targeting. We did extensive research on all of the Sharks prior to the show and a few things stood out about "Mr. Wonderful" that we felt made him a great match as a business partner: (1) he scrutinizes especially hard those entrepreneurs asking for larger investments (his investment in CertifiKID is in the top five in value that he has ever done in ten seasons); (2) he likes businesses that make money and are conservative with expenses; (3) he is all about teaching kids and parents how to save money; (4) he loves female-led businesses; and (5) he has done several investments that intersect with our core market—the mom and family space.

We had limited time to negotiate, and I felt we should focus on doing a deal with the Shark we thought best understood our business and could be the strategic partner we needed. Therefore, in the whopping thirty seconds we had to talk to each other under our breath and the lights to determine our strategy, I suggested this approach to Jamie. She looked at me and said, "Go ahead, I trust you." I turned, looked directly at Kevin, and delivered our counter.

Of the three offers, Barbara asked for the most equity (25 percent) and wanted to turn CertifiKID into a franchise model (which was extensively discussed during our time in the Tank but didn't make it into the episode), which wasn't of interest to us. And while Daymond asked for the least amount of equity (17.5 percent), it wasn't clear why and how he thought he could help us. Meanwhile, we felt Kevin "got it" right away. This context was clear during the Q&A but also didn't make it into the episode.

I knew Kevin is historically a very tough negotiator, so I felt I needed to move quickly into a focused exchange with him in response to his 20 percent offer with a liquidation preference. In doing so, Daymond took himself out as he felt we had come into the Tank looking for a deal with Kevin.

Having watched many *Shark Tank* episodes, my sense is that people often don't fight hard enough. I understand why, as the experience is quite intimidating and you always hear the Sharks say, "Don't negotiate" or "If you don't accept, I may change or withdraw the offer," so there is clearly a risk. However, in my legal practice, I do a lot of negotiating (and have learned a lot from my mentor Michael who is a master negotiator), so I was in my comfort zone.

When Kevin included a "liquidation preference" provision as part of his offer, I was confused. This provision meant that if we sold the company for less than the valuation on which he was investing, he would get his money back off the top before allocating the proceeds based on membership interest. Given his offer was for less than 50 percent of our asking price (and thus valuation), it was quite a rich provision to suggest. Plus, our asking price was rooted in a strong history of revenue and profitability. In other words, we were not a start-up and had been a profitable business for almost ten years with $30+ million in revenue. The risk of us selling out for below $3 million after he invested in us was of course very low. But for some reason, he was stuck on this provision, and I ended up spending a lot of my negotiating capital getting him to drop this idea.

I later learned from his #2, Alan, that while he and Kevin were having breakfast the morning of our taping, they were talking about ways to protect their initial investment in a company where they didn't have control if the goal ultimately was trying to get out and sell cheap. Alan raised the liquidation preference concept and Kevin liked it. So, it was in his head when he rolled it out later in the day as part of his offer to us, which was the first time he had ever included that provision in a *Shark Tank* offer! I said to Alan that I didn't understand why he was hung up on it as it wasn't a fit for our business. He smiled and said, "It made for good TV, right?" In other words, there was no rhyme or reason to his approach. He was mixing it up after a long day of pitches and we were the guinea pig. And my reaction and taking him on about it was good TV.

When I saw the opening, I tested fighting a bit to see how it would be received. When it seemed like Kevin was embracing it, and even respecting it (at one point proclaiming, "I'm loving you" and "I like your negotiating style, you're honest, you're fair"), I felt invited to push a bit further for the deal we wanted. (Jamie told me after that she was afraid that he was going to kick me out and say, "You're dead to me!")

I said, "This is a great deal for you . . . you will make money right away . . . you are getting a great premium on this money already . . . don't let *US* walk out of here over 1 percent . . . my family is going to come in and tackle you (which really got some laughs from the Sharks—this segment is used to this day on CNBC as a lead-in to *Shark Tank* reruns)." After all this back and forth and all my arguments, he then moved 1 percent (just 1 percent!), and said "19 percent."

I know it looked like I was trying to get blood out of a stone in the end by haggling over 1 percent, but my goal was to get Kevin to go to 17.5 percent equity (with no liquidation preference) from his 20 percent initial ask (plus liquidation preference) and he just wasn't moving. If you've watched the show, you know he doesn't move off his initial offers very often.

Although $600,000 for a 19 percent stake in CertifiKID, a $3,157,894 post-money valuation, was a bit more than we wanted to give up, getting Kevin to come down at all from his initial ask (and to drop his liquidation preference) was a victory. Plus, our internal bottom line was 20 percent, so we were at least under that number as well.

I knew I was out of rope, and it was time to accept. When Kevin said "19%," I paused and said "done." He got up and then I realized I wanted Jamie to be the one to accept, so I said to her, "You have to say it." Taken aback, she said, "Say what?" I whispered, "It's a deal," and then she said, "It's a deal!" Kevin clapped his hands, and you could hear Mark Cuban say "Mazel tov!"

Kevin came up to us and gave us a hug and I said, "Kevin, we're going to kill it." Holding hands on our way out, we were pumping our fists for the cameras saying, "We can't believe we got Mr. Wonderful!" We then did about fifty takes of our post-interview, which they ended up playing about five seconds of. We were just tired and drained.

* * * *

So how did we get to this point when many others had failed? How did we get into and graduate with honors from the Harvard of entrepreneur reality shows? By playing the odds and doing all the little and big things to put ourselves in the best position to get where we wanted to go, by taking it all seriously, by being uber-diligent, by cutting corners only if and when we could—that's what we did from the beginning until the end of the process.

WE SAY: Think of your "NO REGRETS" decision (ours was *Shark Tank!*), and JUST DO IT.

We are constantly asked if we are glad that we went on *Shark Tank*. We can say with 100 percent transparency that YES, we look at this as a good decision. Was it the most insane and stressful situation we have ever put ourselves in? YES! But the memories and experiences we have had from it as a business, family, and couple are priceless. The impact it has had on our business is enormous and only continues to pay off. We have a rerun every month, which we consider to be the gift that keeps on giving.

We waited and waited and waited . . . and then the time seemed right . . . and we went for it! Timing + risk = "wonderful" reward.

YEAR 10

All Paths Lead to Mr. Wonderful

SHE SAID: You will never go viral, even after landing on television.

It was March 15, 2019, and as fifteen of my daughter's friends were arriving for her tenth birthday scavenger hunt party, I received the email that I had been waiting for: our *Shark Tank* episode was airing on April 7, 2019. The exhilaration shot through my body like lightning, and I screamed "YES!" with delight, clenching my fist. It was finally about to happen!

By this time, eight months had passed since the taping, and we couldn't tell anyone anything. It was as if I were pregnant and could never tell a soul until after having the baby.

Those days preparing for the airing were hectic and adrenaline-filled as the team and I prepared to make sure our site could handle the traffic, take advantage of getting as much paid advertising as we could as well as local deals, deal with all the PR opportunities and plan a 200-person watch party. Our business generated 150 new deals and $160,000 in paid advertising in those two weeks!

As we were swamped with all these preparations, we also received a call from the ABC television show *The View*, telling us we were going to be featured on an upcoming show with the Sharks as Kevin O'Leary's top deal of the year. We needed to be in New York City for the LIVE show four days after our *Shark Tank* episode airing. We would also need to design a set for this. Are you kidding me?

Somehow, everything came together, and we knocked it out of the park. In true CertifiKID style, we held a family-friendly watch party for 200 of our family, friends, team members, and business partners at a large local indoor play place designed to feel like you are outdoors. They set up a huge screen and lawn chairs and pillows on the "grass" for us and our guests to watch the show. A local TV weather anchor was our emcee for the evening. We had a photo booth with the Sharks' heads for our guests to take pictures with, games and activities for the kids, and an ice cream sundae bar. Everyone was fueled with excitement to find out if we got a deal. Remember, we still had not been able to tell anyone a thing!

I was nervous to see how they would edit down our hour presentation and Q&A with the Sharks into ten minutes of TV viewing time. In the end, Brian and I were generally pleased with what aired. The best part of the night was when we got the deal and a massive balloon drop floated down from the ceiling, and everyone, especially the kids, went wild. It was like we had won the Super Bowl. Then, to close out the night, we announced that everyone should tune in a few days later to see us on *The View*, and they went wild again.

Still on a high, we headed up to New York City on Wednesday night for our appearance on *The View* the next morning. Our director of marketing Kim joined us for this experience. We had a casual dinner with friends that night and then worked on our short script until midnight—we were very nervous about the show being live and the potential need to ad lib in the Q&A with the hosts.

We arrived at ABC studios the next morning and were taken to a green room. Each of the Sharks had selected one business as their favorite deal of the year to appear with them on the show, and we were honored to be Kevin's selection so soon after our show aired. The other entrepreneurs were all friendly and excited. I recognized them all since Brian and I had watched the show religiously that season. We were clearly the newbies.

We were sent to hair and makeup and then taken to the set for rehearsal. This is when we realized we were NOT prepared enough. With *Shark Tank*, I was solid in our pitch and practiced nonstop. But we had been so busy with the airing, I had not had time to get comfortable with our short script for our appearance on *The View*. I started to freak out and revise what we were saying only minutes before going live.

When we got back to the green room, we were greeted by Kevin's assistant, Nina, who we were meeting in person for the first time. She was super cute and friendly but also had a "don't mess with me" vibe. We also learned that Mark Cuban was sick and was not going to make the airing, so Kevin was going to have to fill in for him with his entrepreneurs, which meant less prep time with us.

When show time arrived, we were taken to the set and met with Kevin for a few minutes. He greeted us with a hug. We quickly discussed our segment, and then were ready to roll. No extensive prep for this one! We managed to make it through in one piece and headed backstage. I was really excited to meet Whoopi Goldberg, and we got a great picture with her! We then got a chance to talk to the other Sharks. Barbara joked with us and asked, "Why would you do a deal with that guy?" We took some photos and bolted out of there dying to check on the website traffic to see the impact from the airing.

Brian, Kim, and I ran to a nearby diner for lunch and I whipped out my laptop. We were able to watch the Web traffic in real time from the West Coast airing. Our team told us that the traffic from the East Coast airing was off the charts, with way more traffic and email sign-ups than we saw even from *Shark Tank*! It hit us that *The View* demographic was more in our sweet spot than *Shark Tank* with the focus on the stay-at-home mom. Sitting at lunch, we watched traffic soar higher and higher as the West Coast airing began and felt both thrill and relief. We signed up 12,000 subscribers during that week alone! It was quite a successful and gratifying week which I guess we didn't screw up!

* * * *

Meanwhile, back home in DC, our kids' elementary school principal had declared it "Shark Tank Week" at the school in honor of our family being on the show. They decorated the school with sharks and all the kids made signs about the show that hung throughout the halls. They asked me to come in to speak to the kids about my experience.

I remember that day seeing all the kids' wide eyes and excitement and trying to sit still. As they watched a video of us on the show, they kept looking back and forth between the screen and at me. I found my kids in the crowd, who seemed to share a common reaction of being both embarrassed by the attention but also loving it at the same time. Once the kids finished watching, they turned to me with their questions, some of which were incredibly insightful for elementary school-aged kids.

As I was leaving, one boy even brought over an autograph book for me to sign, which melted my heart. With all the guilt I held over the years for not being able to volunteer in my kids' classes to help teachers sort papers, organize Valentine's Day parties, and be the Girl Scout troop leader, these moments were ones I cherished. They wiped the guilt away for the moment and made me feel like I was still making an impact on these children in my own way. My kids could also feel good about their mom.

* * * *

A month later, still on our high, we headed to Miami where Mr. Wonderful was hosting his annual summit for his *Shark Tank* entrepreneurs. We had no idea what in the world to expect when we arrived at this swanky and chic South Beach hotel and headed to the pool area to meet up with everyone.

There were about sixteen businesses represented, and each had two people attending from their company. It was a diverse group, to say the least. Everyone was decked out in their company garb and super friendly. I recognized the popular Wicked Good Cupcakes and Lovepop Cards entrepreneurs, as they had been showcase companies for Kevin for many years (he always mentioned them during *Shark Tank* episodes).

Once we were all settled into a conference room, we were provided with a rundown of what the week would entail. Our table was in the front row, and we were seated next to a teenager and his dad who started the Lego glue business, Le-Glue. Talk about impressive.

We learned that *Shark Tank* would be filming the summit, which meant this event had turned into another reality show experience. What had Brian and I gotten ourselves into? Everything would be filmed from the full group sessions to our one-on-one time with Kevin to our evening festivities.

An extremely amusing part of the experience for me was watching entrepreneurs from a couple of the businesses constantly hovering around and vying for Kevin's attention and trying to get as much television visibility and iPhone pics as they possibly could. I think Brian and I were just too naive or clueless as this point to realize the self-promoton opportunity that was staring us in the face.

The last night included a big, fancy dinner where O'Leary Wine was featured. I thought I was dressed for the occasion but many of the women entrepreneurs were dressed like they were going to the Oscars. When we arrived, we spent a good amount of time talking to Kevin about the wine and trying different selections. We then noticed there were name tags designating where everyone would sit for dinner. Guess who got the rose, or the seat next to Kevin, that evening? ME! Much to the disappointment of many in the room, I'm sure.

We left the summit feeling like it was such a cool and worthwhile experience. We managed to get some good one-on-one time with Kevin and his team, made some great new contacts, and felt ready and excited to finally get back to work after riding this wave!

As we settled into work again after two months of being on a *Shark Tank* high, I realized we'd better take advantage of all this opportunity quickly. It was not like we had won the lottery and could just sit back and see what happened. Instead, I looked at it as if we had been given a push on the swing and it was now up to us to pump our feet to get us even higher.

Some of the benefits we found from the show were an increased subscriber base (though not as much as I had hoped for and envisioned would be possible back in "the year of the bitch"); name and brand recognition, which greatly helped with getting paid advertising; and new opportunities that seemed to regularly present themselves and kept the team excited.

Every time our *Shark Tank* episode reruns on CNBC, which is about once every two months, we always get a mini spike in subscribers and a few calls from friends saying they just saw us again on TV (which makes us feel like celebrities for a minute). Through Kevin, we even got the chance to film a series with Facebook and Tan France in February 2020! The opportunities just kept rolling in and life was feeling good.

HE SAID: Treat any new partnership like a marriage, not a one-night stand.

What they don't make clear to you when you go through the *Shark Tank* process is that if you tape a *Shark Tank* episode, there is no guarantee that it will air. And if it does air, there is no guarantee it will be in the season you taped. For example, those businesses that taped in June air in the fall and winter. Those that taped in September and October will air in the spring with the last episodes airing in May. During our season, *Shark Tank*'s tenth anniversary season, it wasn't even clear if the show would get renewed for an eleventh season until AFTER our show aired.

Despite these uncertainties, while no one told us this, our research and intelligence suggested to us that if we did a deal on the show, and closed on our transaction, this would increase our odds of getting aired. The producers emphasize that they need just as many "deals" as "no deals," but the show does want the handshake deals on the show, which is all that they are, to close and become actual deals. And the Sharks want this too. But this doesn't mean closing on the deals is easy. It is said that less than 50 percent of the handshake deals close, though the numbers have been increasing over the years. It is also said that about 50 percent of tapings get aired. It's all about playing the odds.

From Jamie's and my perspective, we weren't going through everything we did just for the TV infomercial. We wanted the deal. We wanted a strategic partner to help us take the business to the next level, though not on any terms (i.e., we weren't desperate). But we played the odds. We got the deal. Then we negotiated the terms with O'Leary's team and external counsel. Luckily, my buddy Doug, our legal counsel, stepped in and led the negotiation for us. This was our first external investment, so our corporate and tax structure needed to be adjusted. Key issues for them were Jamie's salary and wanting the ability to approve key decisions that would require substantial investment. It was a challenging and deliberative process and took six months, but we finally got it done and closed on March 1st.

Once they reported internally to *Shark Tank* that the deal had closed, we could sense the momentum, and then two weeks later, we got our air date of April 7th. Just in the nick of time.

Jamie and our team did an incredible job planning the watch party. We had all our family, friends, team, and many business partners there. No one knew for sure if we got a deal or not but obviously assumed it had gone well if we were having a 200-person watch party.

Because when the Gods giveth, they taketh away, our website crashed during the episode from all the traffic. It was really nice when after the episode aired, Alan, Kevin's #2, texted me and said, "Your website is down." Grr . . .

We had done enormous prep for the night with multiple backup servers, which was what everyone was advising us to do because of the expected shower of site activity. Despite all of this, the site still went down, which shows the impact of the *Shark Tank* audience. Notwithstanding this blip, we ended up getting more than 10,000 subscribers between the EST and PST airings. And we learned. We were even more overprepared for *The View*, and every *Shark Tank* repeat we have had since, and we have never had another crash.

Our segment was the last of the four in our episode, so it aired in the last fifteen minutes of the show that started at 10:00 p.m. EST on a Sunday night. Jamie and I were schmoozing and taking pictures during much of the episode before our segment was about to come on. We sat next to each other in two chairs on the left side of the front row and held our breath. It was both exhilarating and horrifying watching the segment. We were in the Tank for the taping for about one hour from start to finish. They edited that hour down to ten minutes, so you have no idea if they will make you look good or bad, smart or dumb.

We obviously knew we got a deal and hoped the show and Kevin would want us to come across favorably to help our business, in which he was now an investor. But it's a TV show after all, so they want to lean into the drama. Immediately after the taping and for the next few days, I relived every moment in the Tank, questioning if we (and I) had done the right thing or said the right thing, hoping we represented ourselves and the company well, and praying that's how it would look on TV to the audience. It was self-torture. And by the time of the airing eight months later, it was all a blur.

There was one moment during the taping when Barbara was making her offer where I had a nervous giggle. Barbara's offer was much more than Daymond's (25 percent versus 17.5 percent) but had a condition that we convert the business to a franchise. She made this offer even though we made clear we had considered that idea over time and did not think it was a good fit for our business, given our desire to maintain total control over our brand and willingness to invest in growing our team nationally. Kevin even said, "Barbara, have you ever heard of an employee?"

Despite this exchange, she still made it a condition of her offer, hence my giggle. She heard it and said, "don't laugh." I immediately fell on my sword and said, "I'm very sorry, I meant no disrespect, and we very much appreciate your offer." She seemed satisfied with that, but Jamie said afterward that she was horrified by it and was wondering if they would air it, which would make me look like an asshole. So, we were both freaking during the airing about that issue.

We sat on the edge of our seats as the show came out of commercial and the music played. There we were on TV, walking into the Tank hand in hand. Jamie said, "Hello Sharks, I'm Jamie Ratner, CEO & Founder of CertifiKID." Then I said, "And I'm Brian Ratner, President of CertifiKID. We're from Potomac, Maryland." And off we went. The room was silent.

During the segment, as our kids were surrounded by their friends treating them like movie stars for their short cameo in the front of the rollercoaster, Jamie and I squeezed each other's hands, I put my head in my hands, and laughed, winced, stressed, and ultimately exhaled when Jamie said, "It's a deal!" Balloons fell and the room was euphoric. People rushed up to congratulate us and tell us how great a job we did. They were particularly buzzing about my negotiation with Kevin. The editing really played it up and made it very dramatic (i.e., good for TV).

When the dust settled, we packed up and got home around midnight. Jamie had taped the episode and we watched it again in our bed with our kids. Without the crowd and distractions, we were able to really focus on how it went and objectively assess how we thought it would be received. At the end, while we both had points we were nitpicking about, such as why did they cut me off here or there, or not include that other thing we said or an entire exchange, we agreed it came out pretty well. And they DIDN'T show me laughing in Barbara's face! Thank God.

We immediately started reviewing social media, which was largely favorable but there were of course some haters. They thought we looked like entitled yuppies with matching outfits. They did not understand the trouble I went through for 1 percent especially when Daymond had offered 17.5 percent. I explained my thinking on this issue above.

We also got some heat online about a point Kevin brought up during the negotiation regarding our customer information and its value to our business. In other words, he suggested that the true value of our business was our customers' data, which we needed to find more ways to monetize; and our response suggested we wouldn't be careful with this data and would sell it to the highest bidder. This was discussed much more extensively during the Q&A, but didn't make it into the episode.

The discussion was based within a much broader context of how CertifiKID is a resource for families and a great partner for businesses whose core audience is the mom-family space. It's these relationships that enable us to offer incredible deals to our subscribers every day. We, of course, take great care with our subscribers' information and in following our Privacy Policy, and we always will. We truly value our subscribers' loyalty, which we know is all about their trust in us and their experience on our site, and we will always remain committed to honoring this trust. This is an example of how, with just some slight editing or by presenting a segment without the entire context, inaccurate impressions can come across to a viewer.

In addition to the successful launch party and the thousands of subscribers we added that night, the other good news for me was that some on social media were playing up my negotiation with Kevin as one of the best negotiations in *Shark Tank* history. During our segment, Kevin posted on social media the following: "I love when the fish start to get sharky. I want to invest in an entrepreneur who can hold their own in the boardroom, even if I'm not there! #certifikid." Nice!

After our episode finally aired and we were able to come out of the shadows, we got to work more closely with Kevin and his team. As Jamie explains, we saw him three days later in NYC for *The View* appearance, which was quite the cherry on top of the whole experience. The fact he picked us out of all his *Shark Tank* businesses was exciting and humbling.

Our segment on the show was literally one minute, and Jamie and I bombed the rehearsal, so we were sweating bullets because it was LIVE. When we were up, because of the way the questions were asked, Jamie and Kevin answered them, and I didn't get to say anything, so I felt a little like a potted plant.

But then, right before they went to the next Shark and their favorite new business, I did the big reveal we had planned and turned around where the back of our CertifiKID sweatshirts said, "Feelin' Wonderful." The camera did a closeup and Kevin and the audience loved it. They also did a closeup of me doing a little jiggle and shaking my ass. Jamie almost lost it. So basically, turning around and shaking my ass was my contribution to our live appearance on *The View*. Whatever it takes to help the business!

Luckily, we headed off on a spring break trip to Mexico two weeks later for some much-needed R&R. Thankfully, we had no business crises happen during the trip and even felt a little like celebrities for a moment at the airport when someone came up to us and said they'd seen us on *Shark Tank* and were big CertifiKID fans. That was cool, and to this day, never gets old!

Two weeks after our break, we traveled down to Miami for Kevin's *Shark Tank* entrepreneur summit, which also was great timing as we were able to spend more quality time with him and his team. Since we were the newest members of the O'Leary family, we got some special treatment and were like the shiny new objects.

Jamie is an introvert, so I know it helped that I was there to facilitate all the schmoozing during our time with the other entrepreneurs. It felt like an entrepreneur workshop and was both informative and inspiring. We bonded in particular with two other couples: Wicked Good Cupcakes (cupcakes in a jar, which was one of Kevin's first royalty deals that he always talked about on his show as being one of his biggest success stories) and Wine & Design (franchise for painting classes for parents where wine is served as a fun night out).

In both cases, the wife ran the business and was the face while the husband was behind the scenes and had another job, though they ran the business as partners. Both had raised or were raising kids while growing their business at the same time, and it was a family affair for them, too. In other words, they were ParentPreneurs, just like us. Obviously, we had a lot we could relate to with each other.

Less than a year later, given we had recently been working together on some partnership ideas, the Wine & Design couple invited us to Raleigh, North Carolina, for the launch of their awesome new headquarters space where Kevin was going to come down, do a big toast, and they were going to do local TV interviews and photo shoots, some of which we could participate in. After the event, we went to dinner with them and Kevin and Alan, which was fun, and we got even more personal time. Just talking to Kevin about our plans, challenges, and opportunities and getting his insights and guidance on that informal level was valuable. He has walked all the paths we are walking, so drawing on his experience was huge for us.

To this day, people always ask us how Kevin is as a partner. When we struck the deal, we believed that having the O'Leary team join the CertifiKID family would open doors and create opportunities for CertifiKID to be the go-to resource for family fun and experiences across the country. His listeners and audience are ours. His mindset is in perfect tune with ours. We felt the sky was the limit and we were truly feeling "wonderful."

And the fact is that it had a big impact on our national exposure, which positioned us well to finally be able to scale our brand. Also, when we need his strategic advice, he and his team provide it, which is a resource we never had before, and few have. As entrepreneurs running our first business, I have always struggled with the concern that we don't know what we don't know.

Kevin and his team know a lot. So just their questions help us focus on areas and issues we may have overlooked, which is an intangible value that we need at this time heading into our next phase and know we will greatly benefit from down the road. But Kevin is involved in a million different projects, so we are very selective and strategic with his and his team's time and have the benefit of not needing that much of it, given how mature a business we are.

Moreover, the reality that a *Shark Tank* appearance and deal with Mr. Wonderful wasn't going to, by itself, answer all of our prayers wasn't such a shock or letdown to us. We knew this was now a marriage (which we had some experience with), and we had to play the long game.

**WE SAY: No one knows your business better than you,
but that doesn't mean no one else can help you grow
your business—understand the difference!**

After the whirlwind of the show (*Shark Tank*) airing, *The View,* and Kevin's summit, we kept waiting for everything to explode. While we clearly had an exciting few months, the reality set in after the summer that the opportunity with Kevin, *Shark Tank,* and the newfound exposure would be what *we* made of it. No one would hand it to us on a silver platter.

When we went on *Shark Tank* seeking a "strategic partnership," we thought maybe we lacked some sort of expertise that someone else who has run a billion-dollar business had. We learned that no one is going to be more of an expert on your business than you. When you are consumed by something 24/7 for years on end and weave it into everything you see or read, there is likely no one else who is going to be able to give you an idea that will be "lightning in a bottle" and magically change your vision or trajectory.

However, there are people who are experts at running successful businesses or who have specific experience with key elements of your business who can guide you and help you grow. Stop looking for a magic bullet and instead focus on different aspects of your business and how those can be improved.

YEAR 11

Part 1: Hoping We Don't Have to File Chapter 11

SHE SAID: When faced with a pandemic, think "puppy" and "pivot."

Instead of building on all the momentum from our *Shark Tank* appearance and deal with Kevin O'Leary and planning our tenth anniversary celebration with all the bells and whistles, we were faced with a once-in-a-lifetime global pandemic and economic collapse. Lovely timing.

It was March 2020 and this new virus that emanated from China called Coronavirus (COVID-19) was all over the news. We had been living in our insulated bubble from January through early March as the virus spread across Asia and Europe, but then the bubble seemed to burst overnight.

It started with the kids being sent home from school and told to bring all their stuff with them. They would be off school indefinitely. Businesses were starting to close. Grocery store shelves were empty. Panic was setting in all around us. What the hell was happening? With a background in security and crisis management, I had always thought of all the emergencies we could possibly deal with, but a global shutdown caused by a once-in-a-century pandemic was not on my list.

A couple of days after the kids were sent home from school, we saw our sales almost completely stop—literally down to like $100 per day. We typically would be selling $15,000–$20,000 in deals per day at this point in the year.

I had anxiety that was eating me up and so many questions about what to do. How long could we go without sales? What did this mean for all the businesses we work with if they were shut down? It was only mid-March but what about all the summer camp deals we had already sold? Was there any chance this would extend into the summer? Most people were thinking it would maybe last a few weeks, or months at the absolute worst. The idea of anything longer was not something most people could even imagine or face, though my background told me this was going to be a much longer and bumpier ride.

With nowhere to go and nothing to do, Brian and I went around and around coming up with a contingency and survival plan for our business which was, of course, based on the concept of family experiences outside the home. With everything shut down and thus no family experiences happening, it didn't take a rocket scientist to realize that we were going to be impacted drastically for an extended period. We decided to act very quickly because every week we went on as normal was another week we were going to put ourselves in a worse position.

We had to do the following:

1. **Cut costs, but be transparent with our employees so they understood what we were doing and why;**
2. **Pivot to new sources of revenue and seek any available government assistance for businesses like ours, but also try to find ways to help our communities; and**
3. **Take care of ourselves and our family.**

Cut costs.

We decided right off the bat we needed to cut salaries and furlough some employees. Doing this on top of all the anxiety in the world created an environment that was like an episode of *Survivor* with the cast of *The Real Housewives*! I was struggling with how on earth to even manage this process.

At one point, there was a terrible group chat going on amongst our team that was getting out of control, so I immediately asked everyone to get on a call. Voices were raised, and the tears started to flow. The sales team was freaking out because they knew they would be the first to be cut or lose their salaries since they had a big commission element to their compensation and thus knew they needed to perform to stay. We needed them to bring in paid advertising to help sustain the business during this time.

We soon realized that the more open and honest we were with the team, the more confident they would feel about their personal situations. Plus, we wanted them to know that I was taking zero salary, so we were all sharing in the sacrifice.

I think many companies in the early phase of the pandemic were taking their foot off the gas and just waiting to see what would happen on the other side when it all blew over. I took a different approach and felt this was the time the team needed to be working hard to make things happen. I knew it was challenging on many levels with clients not in their offices, furloughed contacts, businesses with no money, and the reality that the kids were home 24/7 for essentially our entire team.

I also believe having something to focus on other than the scary news which we had no control over was good for all of us and I wanted them to know we were not going to throw in the towel. I have never been one to wallow in pity (which I got from my mom), as it does no good. We only have control over how we handle adversity, so I needed to make sure everyone on my team had this mentality. We did not have any time here for a pity party.

Pivot.

It was clear we now needed to focus on what parents wanted and needed from home. I pulled off everything from the website that did not make sense right now. No one wanted to be looking at trampoline parks when they were not open; it made them angry and reminded them of the old normal. We started to transition the sales team to focus on experiences we could sell that parents could do from home.

We filled the site with "date night in a box," arts and crafts kits, online coding classes, virtual birthday parties, and the like. I jumped on the phone with "The Great Zucchini" to get him to do a virtual magic show offer which he could now run nationally, as opposed to just locally, to get his name out. It was all about getting creative.

Months later, as some things started to open in the summer, we added experiences into the mix like drive-in movies and fruit farm picking. There were companies who were killing it in the pandemic, such as grocery stores and food delivery, and we made sure we were pursuing them to secure advertising dollars and deals that would keep our audience engaged.

But it was devastating to watch many of our partners temporarily or permanently close their doors, people we had worked with for years: classes, camps, restaurants, events, getaways, amusement and water parks, theaters, bowling, movies, gymnastics studios, trampoline and rock-climbing places, and more. We wanted to help and support them to get through this time. We suggested ideas to them to keep them relevant and tried to help them find ways to pivot, but this proved to be the final straw for many of them—some just had to pull the plug.

When summer rolled around and we were still on lockdown, the refund requests for all the camp and vacation deals we had sold pre-pandemic started rolling in—my biggest fear coming true. The good news is that I had always been so nervous about something like this happening that we had not pre-paid the camps and so had the funds to process the refunds. If we had not taken this approach, this would have really put us in the red.

Take care of ourselves and our family.

Throughout this pandemic, we needed to constantly make sure we and our family were okay. It was our daughter's birthday at the end of March and her birthday was always a big deal to her. At this point in the pandemic, no one had yet thought about how to celebrate birthdays or other special occasions, so I decided to test the waters.

I put together a surprise Zoom birthday party and invited everyone from far and wide to jump on. My daughter got on and was HORRIFIED! She thought it was awkward and strange to just stare at everyone as they wished her a happy birthday. At this point, few knew how to even use Zoom. It didn't help that her grandma could not get herself off mute and I didn't realize there was another page of friends on the call who we didn't even acknowledge. It just sucked and added to our anxiety.

The kids had also been asking for a dog for as long as I can remember, but the chance of us getting one had always been zero. I think it is clear at this point that Brian and I barely had a second to breathe, let alone take care of a pet. However, I was not thinking clearly, and some sort of switch went off that I felt a dog might be the one thing that could get us through this terrible pandemic. I gave the kids the green light to do some research, which kept them occupied for a few weeks, a nice distraction since we were stuck at home with no school or activities outside of their phones and Xbox. They put together a PowerPoint presentation and tried to close the deal. We taught them well!

Before I knew it, I had agreed to getting a white Cavapoo puppy named Zoomie (perfect name after the Zoom phenomenon of this pandemic AND the fact he does these crazy zoomies all the time running around in circles at lightning speed!). We didn't have a clue what we were doing, as neither Brian nor I had ever taken care of a dog. We also had not truly considered how life outside a pandemic would function with a dog under our roof. But at that moment, we did not care. We all fell madly in love with our little fluff ball and Zoomie became the center of our family's universe. He was good for all of us.

We obviously had the time at home to focus on potty training (though we sucked at it!) and learning how to take care of a dog. We were taking him out essentially every hour, and it forced us to wake up earlier and get some fresh air. Outside of Zoomie, during those first few months, our days included lots of family walks, cooking new dishes and family dinners, virtual yoga, and family TV time. And, of course, for Brian and me, work—which never stopped, though at least he was working remotely at home, so we were in the home office all day together.

Our kids never went back to school that year, but the one thing that kept them going was the hope that their sleepover camp would open that summer, which the camp was moving heaven and earth to pull off. And it succeeded (unlike 99 percent of camps)!

* * * *

It was July 9, 2020, and we were driving to New Hampshire from Maryland to drop our kids off at their camp for their miraculous but shortened five-week session, which would be different due to the CO-VID protocols. There were no trips outside camp, no visiting day, and mask wearing for the first week until the bubble was formed and tight. Lila's COVID pre-camp results had not come back yet so we were on pins and needles as she would not be able to get into camp without them. Just as we crossed the New York border and were belting out the soundtrack of *Dear Evan Hansen*, we got the call that she tested negative. Whoo-hoo!

We were feeling very relieved when, just a few minutes later, Brian's phone rang. It was the owner of a business called Macaroni KID.

Macaroni KID is a company with a national digital advertising and experiential marketing platform that leverages its 400+ licensee publishers in communities all over the country who produce hyper-local e-newsletters for their subscribers and are considered the go-to in their communities for all things to do with kids.

We still had a bitter taste in our mouths about the company, as just one month earlier we thought we had reached a deal to acquire their company. We had gotten quite far in the diligence process, close enough that one of the owners told us he would be signing our Letter of Intent ("LOI") the next day. But instead, he called to tell us that, after informing another business that they were proceeding with us, that business suddenly made them an offer they could not refuse. Brian and I spent the next 24 hours trying to decide if we should aggressively go back and try to improve the terms of our offer. Ultimately, after a lot of hand-wringing and a call with Kevin's #2, Alan, we decided not to call him back.

We thus were surprised to get this call. Brian answered, and after some quick pleasantries, the owner said, "Our other deal is dead." Why do all our important moments seem to happen on these drives with our whole family in the minivan? I told the kids to SHUSH so Daddy could talk. The owner said he knew we were disappointed with how things went down last month but he felt this seemed that our deal was meant to be and asked if we'd be willing to come back to the table. He said if we improved our offer in a few manageable ways, they would accept it, but they wanted to hear from us and have a signed LOI in 48 hours or would otherwise have to go down another track.

Our relaxing drop-off in the New Hampshire mountains, and fun with the other camp parents as we all waited nearby for a couple of days to make sure our kids were COVID-free, had just taken a different turn. We needed to not only decide if we wanted to get back in bed with this owner, who we felt had already burned us once and was potentially about to ruin our first semi-vacation in four months, but also answer the slightly larger question of whether we wanted to take on the risk of buying an entire new company in the middle of a pandemic.

Without hesitation, despite the risks and weight of the decision, I knew in my soul I wanted this deal to happen and would not miss out on this second chance. I had been incredibly disappointed when we had lost it the first time and had been thinking nonstop about how I would build a company like this on my own or expand CertifiKID to encompass this model. I believed it was what we needed to scale up and that it would be the perfect complement to our business. The more thought and energy I put into it, the more I realized how hard it would be to do on our own, how much time it would take, and all the value the current business already had.

Therefore, with my not-so-subtle urging, Brian confidently and efficiently negotiated the remaining points of the LOI and got it over the line and signed within their requested time window.

By the time we arrived back home, I was giddy with new energy and excitement about this development. It felt like this could be the piece of the puzzle I had been looking for all these years to take CertifiKID to the next level. I could not believe my good fortune with this deal. Was it my best one yet?

HE SAID: When faced with a catastrophic business event, act quickly and harshly.

You heard from Jamie how our kids conspired in the early days of the pandemic when they had their opening to finally get the dog they had always wanted.

Jamie and I were both the siblings who were not that into our dogs growing up. Our sisters would walk into our respective houses squealing and showering our dogs with love and affection. Meanwhile, we would each walk through the door and barely acknowledge them. Together, we were, therefore, a toxic combination for our kids as we said we would never get a dog. But the pandemic was making people like us do bizarre things. It didn't take long to wear us down and for Jamie to spontaneously say "we'll take him" when a breeder said she only had one Cavapoo left.

Like Jamie, from my perspective, getting Zoomie proved to be a lifesaver for our family and business at a critical time, bringing us joy, love, and a big distraction. He was the first face we saw when we woke up in the morning and the last face we saw when we went to bed at night. Every morning at 6:30, I'd come downstairs and Zoomie would be sitting on Jamie's lap as she smiled and typed away on her laptop—the best pandemic therapy—and I'd feel hope that we would be alright no matter what happened.

I was the least excited and most nervous about the dog. I feared I'd be the one to have to take him out late at night (which I was) and obviously didn't trust our kids to pull their weight. We had a hard enough time taking care of everything on our plate, why would we add something else so significant that we couldn't return? But as I settled into my remote work situation at home, I soon enjoyed the company and the distraction. He'd sit in the office with me and hang out with me, and whenever I was annoyed or stressed, I'd look at him and my mood would change. Jamie took him out the most, and I think she liked how it kept her on the move all day which is just the way she generally likes it.

Prior to the pandemic, I had worked downtown in an office environment for twenty-plus years. To beat the traffic, I'd be out the door by 7:00 a.m. and home after 7:00 p.m. This was what Jamie had to accept and deal with when we met. As you heard earlier, her dad was home by 5:00 p.m. every day, never worked a weekend (until CertifiKID), or went on a business trip. He was at every practice, game, and school event. I was rarely if ever home for family dinner, or to get the kids off the bus. I missed A LOT. Of course, I had regrets about this every day and struggled to find balance between my law practice and the firm I cared deeply about, and my family life.

Travel especially took its toll. I regularly got migraine headaches and had back issues, which I attribute to the stress of my work, travel, and commuting. Jamie never understood me or why I would choose such a challenging career path but she accepted it. She is so independent and capable that, like everything, she just made it all work. I don't think my kids felt that I wasn't there because I would always try to attend everything of importance and was very engaged on the weekends. But they certainly knew I worked all the time. And when we started the business, as you now know, it compounded my workload.

So, when my kids and I were sent home on that Friday in mid-March, I wasn't complaining. I knew I could do my work remotely like I always had successfully done while traveling. And it was somewhat of a relief to not even have to consider commuting or traveling. Pretty quickly, my back felt good, I was less stressed, we embraced family dinners and couples' virtual yoga, long walks around the block with Zoomie, and I loved the quick ten-minute breaks to take Zoomie out and get fresh air.

I took the Steve Jobs approach to my "wardrobe" and basically wore the same thing every day—super comfortable sweatpants, shirt, and hoodie in black, blue, or grey color, and slippers. I didn't wear a tie or button-down shirt for eighteen months. I was the annoying guy who always had a silly Zoom background at the beginning of the pandemic—just to add some levity to the endless video calls.

Like she predicted she would in the early phase of the business, Jamie loved having me home, except for the fact that I stole her office. This led to her moving from table to table throughout the house since she was the one trying to monitor the kids during virtual school, though she didn't complain. And I thought, I could get used to this.

Meanwhile, as Jamie explains, our CertifiKID core business basically went off the cliff in a two-week period as all family experiences outside the home were shut down and people went into hibernation. Overnight, parents were no longer taking trips or going to events, play places, birthday parties, classes, or camps, which was CertifiKID's bread and butter.

Our business partners shuttered, and refund requests started pouring in. Fortunately, because of learning the hard way from all the prior experiences we have spoken about, we had not paid out anyone until the camps, classes, or events started, so we did not have to worry about getting money back from the businesses, which would have been a nightmare (and a fruitless exercise, given their condition). We went into crisis management mode and ran projections for how long we could carry the business if we got to a point where we generated zero revenue.

Kevin had a call with all his *Shark Tank* companies to talk about survival strategies. His first message was to cut expenses as quickly and harshly as possible. His point was you want to benefit from the savings before it's too late, and you can always build back. Second, he implored us to immediately take advantage of the Paycheck Protection Program (PPP), the government program for businesses impacted by the pandemic, because it had the potential to be free money and a lifeline.

Even before the first lockdown in late February, we anticipated a potential COVID impact on our business. As a precaution, we stopped paying Jamie's salary at that time. After everything shut down in mid-March, we closely analyzed what expense-saving measures we needed to put into place. We ultimately decided to cut all nonessential expenses, reduce salaries of team members across the board, terminate one employee, and furlough three others. As Jamie highlights, we tried to be as transparent as possible with our team, so they understood we were in this together and all our decisions were to ensure we survived the impact of the pandemic which was in no way clear.

These were some of the hardest and most difficult decisions we had ever made, and the conversations with employees were heart-wrenching and painful. Everyone was scared and their work and livelihoods depended on us. Luckily, most of our team had been with us for a long time, so we had their trust and confidence, even though they obviously didn't like the painful measures we were taking. But thankfully, they were giving us the benefit of the doubt in dealing with this once-in-a-lifetime business catastrophe.

I was already on top of the PPP opportunity with my father-in-law and CFO, Gary. We studied the program, got legal and accounting advice, and I got our application into my law firm's bank, which was a lifesaver since CertifiKID's bank wasn't set up for the program yet. We made our application on a Saturday, the first day they were taking them, got approved for the money two weeks later, and had the money in our account two weeks after that. This was miraculous, as the program was extraordinarily complicated.

There were literally different interpretations for every PPP provision. And the initial rules incentivized you to spend the money as quickly as possible within eight weeks after you received it so you could get the money forgiven (i.e., not have to pay it back to the bank). As a result, we restored some salaries we had just reduced and brought some people back from furlough. But seven weeks into this period, the rules changed to say you now had twenty-four weeks to spend the money. Ugh! Had we known this, we would have managed the use of these funds much differently and not restored any salaries to get the most out of the money over the longest period. Instead, we ended up having to cut salaries again and put people back on furlough after we spent the PPP money. Lovely.

This is an example of how you just need to roll with it in business situations like this one which are out of your control; make the most prudent decisions you can with the information you have available to you. When we applied for and received a second round of PPP assistance the following year, we had the benefit of the prior experience to draw on and thus were able to effectively maximize the benefit of these funds over a six-month period.

We ended up getting all these funds forgiven, which was key because it gave us the security to not further reduce our employee headcount and to actually start hiring people back. Gary got a big pat on the back from me for rocking the PPP program and getting us this lifeline. I think he too felt a great deal of satisfaction in cracking this complex PPP code.

In addition to cutting Jamie's salary completely and getting the PPP money, I wanted to ensure we had a fallback if we were losing money every month and burned through all our cash reserves, so I secured a personal line of credit. Jamie is very allergic to debt and so was not excited about the prospect of us digging a hole to carry the business for an unknown period.

Therefore, to avoid ever having to tap into the line of credit, Jamie wanted to know what her revenue goal was to break even every month with the salary reductions, furloughs, and expense-saving measures we had put in place. So, we came up with some estimates and she wore that number around her neck as she scratched, clawed, and pivoted our sales team to revenue-generating opportunities, such as paid advertising and "CertifiKID at Home" offerings that she has described.

Her approach worked. We ended up at least breaking even during most months, which was a huge boost, and never had to access the line of credit.

* * * *

When the kids got the green light that they could go to their sleep-away camp in June, we were all beyond excited. We needed a break from each other. Jamie and I needed the summer to refresh and plan for how to ensure the business could stay afloat through the pandemic, which had no apparent end in sight, while the kids needed the opportunity to be with their friends, play sports and activities, and be outdoors in a safe environment.

After our short call with the Macaroni KID owner which Jamie describes in detail, Jamie looked at me, smiled and said, "This is a second chance, and we cannot lose it."

Our relaxing and carefree weekend in the mountains with friends (finally) turned into a stressful whirlwind where we were distracted with the deal and frustrated with the Wi-Fi and cell reception as we talked to our legal counsel Doug and confirmed our decision. But 48 hours after the call, I called the owner and said we were IN. I worked up the new LOI and, after a few exchanges of drafts and negotiating the last remaining open terms, we had a signed agreement by Tuesday.

Our friends were super patient and supportive during the weekend as we were late to every meal and destination. They also proved to be a valuable sounding board on hikes and chill time in the lake, which gave us the peaceful space to make a monumental decision that would forever change our business and future.

Your closest friends, even when they don't live near you or know the intricacies of your work, can be the best counsel and advisers. They know you and understand you like few others.

Remember that if this deal went through, we would be doubling our team overnight and taking over a totally different business model *in the middle of a pandemic* where we had already furloughed or terminated staff and had implemented an across-the-board salary reduction. In other words, this was a BIG risk and investment.

And I knew how much time and energy the process would take, and I'd be responsible for getting it over the line. I'd be working with Doug and his team as they took the lead on the diligence process and drafting the deal documents. They'd liaise with the seller's counsel as well but I knew, given it wasn't a big or complicated deal, there would be an effort by the parties themselves to work out open terms directly to keep things moving and to save costs.

On the drive home on Wednesday, I braced myself as we strategized and planned for the diligence process which would have to take place in a very accelerated period. A big attraction to the deal with us for the Macaroni KID owners was the prospect of a quick close—three weeks. It ended up being four weeks, and the extra week was very stressful and almost resulted in the deal blowing up. Though, for context, one month is actually a short period of time to complete diligence, negotiate and agree on documents, and execute on an agreement of this size, nature, and complexity.

Meanwhile, our kids were living their best lives. Our daughter Lila wrote a letter home to us after the first week when they successfully created the bubble. She said when they announced that everyone had tested COVID-negative and could now take their masks off, "it was one of the best days of my life and like corona didn't even exist." What a gift. It was truly a miracle summer for Jamie and me as well. We went to the beach with Zoomie and worked on the Macaroni KID deal from there.

As our lawyers worked up the deal documents, we dug into the diligence materials, analyzed the numbers and issues, and Jamie and our management team talked to many of the Macaroni KID team members as we tried to figure out who would be joining us post-acquisition as opposed to going with the owners to their other business. All of this had to happen via Zoom and phone obviously. The owners gave us their advice and opinions, but also wanted us to speak to people and make our own decisions.

We sought Kevin and Alan's advice, given their deep experience with acquisitions and integration. Kevin didn't pull any punches. He said we should be prepared for a rough ride, which is typical with acquisitions, and should take fewer people with us than we think we need because it's always easier to hire than fire.

Ultimately, we went with the owners' advice in most situations, as we wanted to send a message to their team and community of continuity so we could have a smooth transition and then see what changes, if any, we wanted to make down the line consistent with our vision. In retrospect, Kevin's advice was prescient, and we'd do some things differently if we had to do it all over again. But we just didn't know what we didn't know, didn't have the time to figure everything out, and needed to get the deal done and everyone over, so we could then look under the hood and see where we wanted to go.

Once drafts of the deal documents were circulated, from our perspective, the owners were difficult and impatient on issues that seemed minor to us, while being flexible and easygoing on the bigger points. This is a good example of how you can't assume you know what the big and small points are to the other negotiating party. I learned later more background and context to their situation which gave me perspective I didn't have then on the "why" of a lot of issues.

The lesson is to treat all terms as significant, determine what is important to you, and spend your capital on those points. If you get some easy wins, take them, and don't overthink it because there probably is a good reason for it. It's impossible to consummate a deal if you're constantly thinking the other side is trying to screw you. This mindset is hard to get across to Jamie who is always suspicious, but this is why she lets me take the lead and just makes sure I know what is important to her.

After negotiating and resolving a few final tricky issues, the documents were in agreed form and ready to be signed. The last challenge was getting Kevin's signature while he was taping *Shark Tank* episodes in Las Vegas. While he had already approved the deal and a close-to-final version of the terms, he still had to review and sign the actual agreement. Alan was a lifesaver by orchestrating time during a taping break for him to review and sign. At 4:00 p.m. on Friday, all signatures were in, and the deal was done.

Our pandemic pivot was complete. Jamie and I took a celebratory walk around the block with Zoomie. We knew the honeymoon would be short and it surely was.

WE SAY: In business and in life, don't let negative events just happen TO you; you must own them so you can find your way THROUGH them.

We could have just sat back and freaked out over what was happening in the world and in our business and slowly let the business wither or die. It could have been our "out" after a decade of blood, sweat, tears, and, yes, success. No one would have held it against us.

However, we never once even let ourselves think that way. We chose to push ourselves and our team to pivot and keep our business relevant, in the black, and alive. We then took our biggest business risk yet with a pandemic pivot acquisition. When faced with negative events, you can either take control of them or they will control you.

· *12* ·

YEAR 11
Part 2: Crazy Like a Fox or Just Crazy?

**SHE SAID: Some of the best opportunities
appear during the worst of times.**

With the acquisition of Macaroni KID, we saw great potential for our combined company, and its headquarters (HQ) team seemed amazing and committed. But we had never acquired people in an acquisition before, and here we essentially doubled our team overnight in the middle of a pandemic.

Let's start with some key background on the business and community we acquired so you can assess if we were crazy like a fox or just crazy.

Macaroni KID is a family-focused digital media platform aimed at providing parents the scoop on the best things to do and places to go with kids in their community. The business includes a national website with parenting content, as well as hundreds of local sites across the country that are run by individual "publishers" (who are mostly moms, but there are a few dads and grandmas as well) in each community who are licensees of the Macaroni KID brand.

Publishers purchase a license for the exclusive right to publish the Macaroni KID site and newsletter for their community and to use the Macaroni KID brand, platform, and resources to run their businesses. This means that a major part of the Macaroni KID operation is focused on recruiting, onboarding, hiring, and providing ongoing support for these publishers, of which there are hundreds across the United States and Canada.

In addition to running their local websites and publishing a weekly email newsletter, publishers also participate as influencers in national advertising campaigns sold by Macaroni KID HQ sales executives.

Major brands partner with Macaroni KID to reach their target audience through authentic, experiential marketing campaigns.

For example, a company like Heinz may have a new flavored ketchup that they want to get in the hands of moms. Macaroni KID offers campaigns where publishers distribute samples of the ketchup to hundreds of local moms. Publishers also produce content that shows moms exactly in which aisle to find the new ketchup in their local grocery store to purchase.

These local influencer-based campaigns are Macaroni KID's specialty. They are super creative and highly successful. This was right up my alley.

We thought this acquisition would be a homerun for the business because this new company had millions of subscribers nationally AND boots on the ground with real engagement within their local communities and with local businesses. Add in CertifiKID's deal piece and we felt the synergy in what the combined entity could offer was unmatched. We were psyched to get moving!

The Monday after our deal closed in mid-August, the now former co-owner wife set up a Zoom call announcing the acquisition to the publisher community. She opened the call by explaining why they had decided to sell after twelve years, why they couldn't tell anyone before now, that they were ready to move on and focus on their other business, and that the community needed a new "mama bear" and we were the right leaders to take the business and community forward. Of course, I was thinking to myself: *How soon before they all realize I'm not the "mama bear" type?*

Brian and I took a deep breath and prepared to deliver our welcome message to the hundreds of publishers about our leadership and vision for Macaroni KID, now that we had taken the reins. We tried to be gracious to the former owners, humble and reassuring, while adding in a mix of some funny, cute, and clever stories and anecdotes about us and our company in the hope that it would resonate with the publishers. Unfortunately, it all fell flat.

We expected a warm welcome but were met instead with quite a heavy dose of skepticism. We were too corporate, too scripted, not real, had ulterior motives, and were essentially the opposite of the former "mama bear" owner who was very inspirational and empowering. It was clear there was going to be resistance and some haters—not even a one-day honeymoon!

Little did we know what was in store for us over the weeks to come. We were in the dark about a lot of recent drama within their HQ team and the community in general and had no idea what this business truly entailed. While we had done extensive due diligence before the acquisition, it was still very compressed into a short period of time and rushed. Peeling back layer after layer after the deal closed was quite eye opening.

About two weeks in, we started to feel we were in over our heads and firefighting every day. What did we just sign on for here? We had been left with the impression that the business largely ran itself, which is why the owners had been able to launch their other new business for a couple of years, while running Macaroni KID. We thought we would be set.

It was not all gloom and doom though. There were glimmers of light and amazement we saw daily. I could not believe what some of these publishers were doing for their communities, especially during these trying times. One of them would get an idea and then share it and, before you know it, they were all rolling it out to their individual communities like an army.

They had started a Boo Basket campaign for Halloween where they put together 100 goodie bags and delivered them to the doorsteps of families to surprise them and encourage them to "pay it forward" to a neighbor. They held drive-thru events for Valentine's Day to give families in their communities some way to celebrate since schools were closed and kids had no way to enjoy holidays. They did little things like helping a new family get oriented when moving to their community.

However, it was hard to focus on all the bright spots when our phone was ringing off the hook starting at 7:00 a.m. and going until 11:00 p.m. with emergency calls from members of the HQ team about roles, personalities, and financial and HR issues. This daily chaos required us to triage from one person to the next every day. They had been through a lot with the transition, and many had been with the business for five to ten years or more. It was as if they had all been suppressing their feelings about their work and value for a long time, and now finally felt liberated to let it all out.

At that time, there were 400+ publishers. The community has a Facebook group where the publishers go to share and connect. I soon realized they were using this forum as the place to comment on and criticize our every move. If we did something they liked, there was a post two minutes later with thirty comments and positive reinforcement. But if they were not happy about something, we got thirty rants, which can be demoralizing.

* * * *

Meanwhile, in our home (but outside our home office), we had our own craziness going on as our kids still were not in school so were doing their classes and work virtually. This required us to be on four Zoom meetings all day in four different rooms of the house. It was nuts. The one thing that was happening outside our home was team sports. During the pandemic, sports leagues took it up about ten notches, realizing families had absolutely nothing else going on besides sports since all other events were on pause. Therefore, on the home front, our kids' lives revolved around virtual school and their travel soccer clubs.

Our daughter Lila's soccer team had just been assigned a new coach. I had grown up playing competitive soccer and lived and breathed the sport until I hit my junior year of high school. After two unbearable years with my high school coach, I broke and had to quit. It had quite a negative impact on my confidence and my teen years. So, you can imagine how I felt when my eleven-year-old daughter was assigned my old coach as her club coach. Could this year really get any crazier?

My first instinct was to remove her from the team. How could I put my own daughter in a position like this? Especially because she was even younger than I had been when I played for him. However, Lila rejected this idea. She loved her soccer team and had been playing with them for years. We discussed it and decided that she could give it a shot, but at any point I would allow her to switch to a new team if it didn't go well and she experienced the kind of anxiety I had experienced playing for this coach.

All year long, we took her to practice four times a week and multiple games on the weekends; they even played through the cold winters. I could barely watch the games without cringing and feeling like my fifteen-year-old self. He was the same coach he had been for decades.

The interesting part was that my daughter thrived. She wasn't me. She grew into the most incredible soccer player beyond my wildest imagination. Did he yell at her and tear her to shreds at times? Yes! Did he play mind games with her and pull her out of games if she was playing poorly? Yes! Did any of this impact Lila to the point she did not want to go to games or practices? Honestly, maybe twice the entire year it affected her confidence, but she fought and played through it. She was tough. It makes me emotional just thinking about it. Turns out, she is stronger than her wimpy mom.

I learned from this experience. I learned a lot about my daughter and about myself, and I gained more perspective. My first reaction was to never even consider letting her play. This really taught me how important it is to not see life through one lens. We always want to protect our children from dealing with tragedy, but if we try to stop them from experiencing things, they will never be able to grow on their own. From this experience, I also started to question who I was and how I saw the world as a teenager. Was I too sensitive? Was I too quick to quit?

* * * *

Thus, 2020 and 2021 were the most stressful years yet.

I guess we should have realized that acquiring a company—any company—in the middle of a health, economic, and racial crisis was going to bring a shitload of issues. All we saw was the great opportunity and we worried about the financial risk. Never did we think we would be signing away the little time we had outside of our business to the whims of hundreds of women from all walks of life across the country who demanded and needed our attention and action for their own livelihoods. These women and this community were crying out for new leadership and inspiration.

Very quickly, our leadership skills and cohesion as a couple and team were put to their greatest test, and we learned many lessons.

1) *When integrating teams, communicate directly and often with every team member and clearly define roles, responsibilities, expectations, and the chain of command.* We were now dealing with two sets of employees that needed to be integrated virtually when we hadn't even met the Macaroni KID team in person yet. Surprisingly, the Macaroni KID

employees were not a cohesive team. Some were in new roles, and all were concerned about their jobs and the future of the business. They feared our goal might be to learn everything about their jobs and then push them out. They questioned if our plan was to just stop their business and use the assets, like the email list.

Meanwhile, I assumed the CertifiKID team would be bursting with excitement about the new opportunities, but they were not. They were concerned about our neglect of the CertifiKID business and them personally, about how the sales platforms could be integrated, and about all the work they now had to do on the volatile Macaroni KID side. My phone rang off the hook from morning until night, and I hate talking on the phone so you can imagine my mood.

But communication is key when you are undergoing any meaningful business change. Each team member needed to know what we expected, who they should report to, what we wanted them to prioritize, and how each segment of the business impacted them (or not). And we needed to reinforce these messages regularly. Candidly, we didn't do a great job of this, so the confusion made the integration more difficult and I'm sure we lost opportunities as a result.

2) *Be upfront with your vision and then let your actions speak louder than words.* I was buying a business. Little did I know this business was not a "business" in the eyes of the publishers but a family and community. That is great, but I acquired a business. Right off the bat, we were met with resistance for trying to treat Macaroni KID more like a business while respecting the culture and community that had been successfully built over the years. Striking this balance felt impossible on a day-to-day basis because people heard what they wanted to hear and didn't trust us.

Ultimately, we simply had to explain what our vision was, and then implement it with action. Some things people liked. Other things people disliked. Some people left but most stayed, as the great majority of the community felt the changes that we were making were long overdue and much needed, even if certain actions didn't benefit them.

3) *Instill your core values.* When we looked under the hood of the Macaroni KID business, we uncovered open wounds related to racial injustice issues that some expressed had not been adequately acknowledged and addressed. Two months prior to our acquisition, George Floyd was murdered, and along with the Black Lives Matter (BLM)

movement, helped propel a national reckoning on racial justice issues. Everyone was struggling with the impact of these issues in their lives, but many businesses were as well. We were no exception. This community was a microcosm of what was happening nationally.

Prior to taking over, we were not aware of the depth of the impact that these issues were having on the Macaroni KID community, though we knew that the community had a Diversity Committee seeking to address the issues and encourage engagement and understanding, as well as a recently formed Black Publishers' Caucus. We also knew that there had been publisher diversity training that we agreed should continue, but the HQ team had not yet had training.

Despite these efforts, we soon learned there were divisions among many publishers, which were being fomented in the Facebook group, as well as frustrations with how HQ was handling these issues. In some of the publishers' minds, fairly or not, the former leadership had not moved quickly enough nor were they visible enough in speaking out on the issues and communicating about what Macaroni KID stood for and was going to do in response. Of course, they were in the process of selling the company, so it was terrible timing for them as well.

We were handed a VERY hot potato and quickly understood that this it a vital issue that we had to address right away. However, it was so complicated, and there was so much emotion wrapped around it, that it didn't lend itself to quick decisions or results. We set up Zoom calls with the Diversity Committee and Black Publishers' Caucus to find out as much as we could and hear them out. These were not short calls and there was no shortage of tears.

Though we learned from them, which greatly helped with our future planning for the combined company, we knew we needed to work toward fixing the inequities that existed, and fast. We needed to increase diversity within the publisher community and HQ team and make it more inclusive and equitable across the board, consistent with our core values.

Even though we were taking a breath before doing any additional hiring (we were in the middle of a pandemic after all), we realized neither we nor anyone on our CertifiKID team or Macaroni KID team had the necessary experience on diversity, equity, and inclusion (DEI) issues. The publisher chairing the Diversity Committee, Zulema, did have this background and had been charged with training the publisher community on these issues. And she was fantastic. We spent a lot of time with her and decided to make her the company's DEI officer. I believe this was one of our best decisions, as all the work we did and the foundation we laid started to ripple throughout our own community and then spill out into the communities we served.

This process and the issues surrounding equity also made us realize that we needed to have all the publishers sign new contracts. The publisher contracts had evolved over the twelve years of the business, so many of the publishers were operating under different terms and rules. Also, few seemed to know what many of the rules even were, and let's just say that enforcement was not always consistent. In December, we announced that we would introduce a new contract on January 1st that everyone would need to sign. If anyone chose not to sign, their existing contract would lapse at the end of January.

This kicked off the shit show to end all shit shows. There were some influential long-standing publishers and ringleaders who knew right off the bat they were not going to sign the new agreement. Instead of leaving quietly and gracefully, they tried to burn the house down on the way out by influencing other publishers to also leave the community.

By the deadline, we ended up losing 100+ publishers through this process, or approximately 25 percent of the community. To keep things extra interesting, I then learned that a core group of them had hatched a secret plan to leave and start a competing business. Several of the Macaroni KID HQ team were also publishers and had strong relationships with many of the publishers who were leaving. They were very emotional and under a huge amount of stress. I am sure they questioned their new owners' choices and leadership. Brian and I knew that, most importantly, we needed everybody on the same playing field for this business and community to run and operate successfully in the future under our leadership.

This was also the same month as the January 6th insurrection and Joe Biden's inauguration as president. The inauguration really hit home with us as we saw how leadership can change and unity can be hard to achieve. Some people will like and welcome the change, and some will not. For those publishers who chose to follow us on the journey, we were very grateful for their confidence and positivity. For those who decided we were not their cup of tea, and it was time to move on, we understood and wished them well with respect and kindness (even the one who told me to rot in hell).

However, through the whole messy process, I kept my eye on the prize because I truly believed that Macaroni KID was the last key piece of the CertifiKID puzzle that we needed to scale our business nationally and more hyperlocally. This was the root of my sense of hope and promise despite the daily challenges.

And it was.

Vaccine distribution began to pick up pace. After over a year, our kids went back to school. Businesses started to open. The contract period was over, we were finally hitting our stride on the Macaroni KID side, the integration of the two businesses was going more smoothly as our team started to jell, and CertifiKID was picking up again as businesses were opening and events were starting back up.

A bunch of event producers started to roll out different themed family shows throughout the country. These were our first shots at seeing whether we could gain any traction selling our tickets in towns like Boise, Idaho, and Birmingham, Alabama—markets where we had never dreamed of selling deals before. To our amazement, the sales flowed in.

I started to feel a ping of joy—of hope—that my puzzle might finally be complete. I know it wasn't like I'd found a cure for cancer, but it was something I had been laser focused on for years and it always seemed just out of my reach. However, it was also anticlimactic. It was like when you are reading a book and almost at the part where the mystery is going to be solved. In one sense, you are excited to find out how it is going to end, but there is a part of you that doesn't want to read that last page.

The sense of satisfaction was short lived though, as I have learned the puzzle is never quite complete. It just grows and you are constantly searching for more pieces. There are more challenges each day. As an entrepreneur, there really is never an ending until you sell the business and walk away.

There are certainly days when I am pushed to the edge, and I think to myself, I am ready and it's time. It has been twelve years after all, and I am human. But most days, I feel lucky and blessed to be able to do something that combines so much of what I love, and that I get to build and run something that I am proud of alongside Brian.

The business has been like our third child. We have nurtured it from birth, put our heart and soul into its growth, and experienced highs and lows, successes and setbacks. And it's not something you can ever give up or let go, even when it evolves into something you didn't envision. You pivot together and keep investing. And then the child becomes this beautiful adult, and you are a beaming Parent(Preneur).

* * * *

A few months later, as the conditions improved with COVID-19 and people started to travel, we had the opportunity to attend our first Macaroni KID Boondoggle in Punta Cana, Dominican Republic. From the beginning, we had heard noise about how amazing these Boondoggle trips are.

Once a year, up to fifty publishers with the biggest subscriber bases are selected for the opportunity to take a trip with all expenses paid (minus their airfare). The hotels and resorts do this as a way of bringing influencers to their properties to promote their experiences. Rumor had it that these trips were often what fueled these publishers all year long as it was a big goal and reward that they were shooting for, so we needed to make sure we kept the tradition going.

Thus, in the summer of 2021, instead of taking our typical week trip somewhere exciting to be together while our kids were away at camp, we joined thirty women from across the country in Punta Cana. We had no idea if they were going to embrace us or spit on us. We headed to the airport, took a deep breath in the car, and psyched each other up that we would do our best and make the most of the experience.

We arrived at the gorgeous resort and were walking to our room when a big trolley full of mom publishers pulled up next to us screaming in delight like we were celebrities. They jumped out and immediately started hugging us and seemed super jazzed to see us. Phew. At least we knew some were excited to meet us.

When we arrived at the big opening night dinner on the beach, we saw many of the faces we had seen over the past year on Zoom and social media. Some of the HQ team members were also on the trip and it was surreal to meet them in person after working so closely together for a whole year. There was an instant feeling of relief to finally see them in person, give them a hug, express our appreciation for their hard work and sacrifice, and to feel each other's true energy.

The Caribbean food and drinks flowed, and we all basked in the tropical air and view of the turquoise ocean. Remember, the only view most people had had for the past year was of their backyard.

Brian gave a nice welcome speech and then passed the mic to me. Honestly, I botched it royally and sounded like an idiot. Brian gave me some buzz words to try to sound inspirational, but it just did not come out that way. I did talk about how I am an introvert, and that it is hard for people like me to be on a trip like this, so I asked everyone to please be kind and inclusive to all my fellow introverts.

For some reason, despite my lack of eloquence, whatever I said seemed to resonate with at least some of the women. They also felt like I was real, just like them. So, just focusing on being myself, I started the trip off successfully. And my lesson to anyone in a leadership and public speaking role is always to just be yourself because you are going to botch trying to be something you are not!

After dinner, it became clear to me that this "Moms Gone Wild" trip (everyone had been cooped up from the pandemic after all!) was going to have plenty of drinking and dancing. There is nothing I am more insecure about than my dancing. Oh geez. Immediately, they pulled me into a circle and wanted me to dance with them. Next thing you know, they brought Brian into the mix and pushed him in the middle to dance. Poor Brian!

One of the publishers indiscreetly asked us what our wedding song was (since they knew it was our seventeenth anniversary the day before). You see where this is going. Toward the end of the night, our song "Truly" by Lionel Richie suddenly came on and Brian and I had no choice but to start slow dancing to our song on the beach! What a night and the start of a crazy trip.

Over the next few days, we had many meals, dance sessions, a chocolate experience, boat cruise and pool parties, and we started to get comfortable with the publishers and learn their stories. They all have different backgrounds, from special education teachers to hospice care workers to those who were Macaroni KID publishers full time and truly making a good living at it. They told us about their communities and the impact they have had on them. For some of them, this was the first time they had been outside the country. They told us about their struggles as parents and challenges in their marriages. We watched as they reunited with old friends and made new bonds. They shared laughs and they shared tears. They shared and supported each other with tools and business advice.

As the layers peeled off, they also peeled off for me. This trip, and finally meeting some of these publishers in person, was exactly what I needed to fuel the fire inside me to push this business and community to the next level.

The Boondoggle trip was reminiscent of our trip to Miami for Kevin's *Shark Tank* summit, where you have a short amount of time and opportunity to bond with a group of new people. We were determined to meet and talk to all thirty publishers there and we succeeded. I took notes at the end of every day and sent an email to the community after the trip where I shared what I learned and loved about every person there. I wanted them to know I was listening and the community to know how fantastic these women are.

After exactly a year of ups and downs and constant turmoil as we took the reins and put 110 percent into making this a stronger business and community, I was starting to wonder how in the world I could keep my stamina going. But meeting these resilient and fabulous women and appreciating the impact this business is having on them and their families, communities, and other business owners truly made me realize that I need to put my foot on the gas. The opportunities are limitless for Macaroni KID; and with CertifiKID coming out of the pandemic with all the pent-up demand for family experiences outside the home, the combined opportunity is enormous.

While I'm a bit scared and overwhelmed about letting everyone and myself down, I know I'm blessed to have the freedom and power to do whatever I think is necessary to realize my vision and make this business the most profitable and successful it can be, valuable and impactful to our communities, and a rewarding and joyful experience for all the members of our team and publishers in our community.

I've gotten this far against the odds.

I wouldn't bet against this ParentPreneur.

HE SAID: As Mr. Wonderful advised, integration of two mature businesses is not a wonderful experience.

As Jamie explains, with most of their core team in place post-acquisition, we were hoping the Macaroni KID business would run itself long enough for us to determine our vision and strategy for the combined business. We also thought the CertifiKID team would see the opportunity and potential as clearly as we did.

Wrong on both fronts.

The Macaroni KID business required most of our attention from day one as Jamie describes. Meanwhile, the CertifiKID team was generally in a foul mood. They were puzzled how we could have acquired another business, doubling our team, while they were on a salary reduction or furloughed. The way some of them saw it was we had used their salaries to pay for the deal and these other people. Also, they felt neglected as we shifted our short-term focus away from them. Sigh.

Against this skepticism, I was responsible for communicating exactly what we were doing and why. We tried to get them to understand that we didn't go looking for the opportunity, but it came to us and had the potential to be a game changer for CertifiKID and all of them. But, of course, we didn't have all the answers on how we would integrate and how the business segments would work alongside each other until we got to know the Macaroni KID team and business better. We asked for patience and understanding from everyone, but both were naturally in short supply.

As we started to learn the business and get to know everyone, we had to plan for their annual Meet Up, which was already in the works when we acquired the company (though this year it was virtual). Meet Up is essentially a publisher retreat filled with learning, education, and inspiration. They also obtain sponsorships for the event and deliver swag bags to all the attendees. Jamie secured Olympic gymnast Dominique Dawes and Washington, DC, CBS anchor Lesli Foster, who were both incredible and inspirational keynote speakers.

Jamie and I did an opening speech for the virtual event, and then moderated and led several other sessions. Jamie's talk was super motivating as she encouraged the publishers to think and act more like entrepreneurs because they are ParentPreneurs too! Overall, we did much better when compared with the first Zoom meeting and seemed to be well received.

At the publisher award sessions where we honored the best publishers and those with the most subscribers, we dressed up as a Deer in Headlights (I was the deer and Jamie was the headlights) which helped take the edge off everyone. And the event was generally a success with positive feedback. We were just happy that we got through it and seemed to meet people's expectations.

Meanwhile, Jamie was working with the team on the Macaroni KID technology and infrastructure. Amie, Bien, and Kim from our CertifiKID team did an amazing job helping us work with the Macaroni KID team to refine and improve their systems, platforms, policies, and procedures across all aspects of their side of the business. The fact that CertifiKID business was slow from the pandemic ironically helped us to have the space and time to devote to this effort and the integration.

And Jamie and Leslie worked with the Macaroni KID sales team to align and build a joint offering. Soon our CertifiKID team saw the potential, as major new and old brand clients alike were signing on to advertising campaigns covering both businesses—$25K here, $50K there, and even a $100K would roll in every now and then. This was BIG business. But many of these campaigns relied on the publishers to write content or reviews so there were always many moving pieces to every campaign.

Jamie was looking at this business with fresh eyes and common sense and trusting her instincts which had never let her (or us) down in eleven-plus years of running a profitable business. This led to streamlining some areas, eliminating redundancies in others, scaling some things up and other things down, though in the first phase, the changes were measured and incremental but signaled a new direction of travel.

As you heard from Jamie, some people loved and embraced the change as long overdue. Others seemed to fight it all, and it often felt personal, though we tried hard to not take things personally. Jamie was better at this than I was. She's Teflon. Meanwhile, I always care what people think.

We'd wake up and look in the Macaroni KID Facebook group in the morning and would hold our collective breath to see if we would have an uplifting or disheartening start to the day. At a certain point,

I couldn't even look. But the bottom line was we were doing what we felt was best for the business as a whole and, while we felt the hits, we weren't going to be deterred.

As Jamie discussed in depth, the new contract bombed with many publishers. They hated that it was nonnegotiable, which I found strange because it's not like any licensor would ever not present a standard license agreement to hundreds of licensees that wasn't subject to individual negotiation. Changes we thought were noncontroversial were very controversial. We knew we needed a Zoom call to discuss the issues so they could hear it from the horse's mouth.

We got lots of feedback from publishers about what to cover on the call, so we tried to do this and be very raw and honest. People were suspicious of our motives, so we tried to explain how and why we acquired Macaroni KID, what our vision was for the future, what we had already accomplished in just a few months, and what we were trying to achieve with the new contract that we wanted *everyone* to sign.

It would be an understatement to say it was a disaster. We took hit after hit as the Zoom chat was essentially a running commentary from the vocal minority of how clueless, unappreciative, and awful we were. Ouch. Of course, we knew the silent majority was with us and would give us a chance, but they were drowned out in this forum by the anti–Jamie and Brian ringleaders. Every day that followed for the rest of the month we fielded calls with publishers, trying to make connections, listening to their concerns, and providing comfort and encouragement about the contract and us personally.

Candidly, we lost more than we thought we would—a quarter of the publishers. It was a blow. But in retrospect, we feel it was for the best. For many that left, it was just their time. They had hung in there for a long time, maybe their kids were now grown, and we were an excuse to finally hand their site over to someone else who would bring in fresh ideas and energy. For others, the reality was that they liked things the way they were and didn't want change. For us, we wanted people in the community who shared our vision, were supportive and positive, and were with us. If they couldn't commit to this, they were likely not going to be a long-term fit for the community under our leadership.

We were confident that we would improve the business and community and help them become more successful and impactful in their community. And we knew that we would be judged by our actions and not our words, but all we asked was that they give us a fair chance. This is a good lesson. You don't want someone on your team who thinks there is an "i" in "team" or who isn't with the owners and leaders. It always ends, and not always well.

Meanwhile, as spring came and vaccines were introduced, it felt like we could see the light at the end of the tunnel. Joe Biden was in the White House and Trump was in Mar-a-Lago. Our kids went back to school in April. We got our PPP2 loan, and the business conditions were finally improving.

The pent-up demand was driving lots of camp deals and events as these businesses opened their doors and had COVID-19 protocols that parents believed were safe and would work. Our ad revenue and voucher sales picked up considerably. The switch went off with the sales team and they now saw the opportunity the same way we did. After a lot of analysis and projections, we fully restored our salary levels across our team (except Jamie, just to be safe) and started looking to hire back some positions to get our headcount closer to where it was pre-pandemic.

Of course, the COVID-19 variants have stalled some progress and prevented us from coming fully out of the tunnel at the time of this writing, but we remain optimistic that our business can get back to pre-pandemic levels by the end of next year 2022, and that we will see growth of our combined business dwarf these levels in the year after that.

And on the Macaroni KID side, the team did a killer job building back up the publisher community in the months after the new contracts were signed to the point where we were at our pre-contract numbers by September and hit our 2021 year-end goal for new publishers.

We started to feel the momentum, enthusiasm, and support, which we finally got a true taste of on the Boondoggle trip. For me, the experience hit home how much we have lost during the pandemic. Human connection. Zooms are better than calls (when the Zoom call doesn't get dropped) but do not replace in-person contact. And we had never met any of these people who joined our team during the pandemic. We also haven't had a meeting with our CertifiKID team in eighteen months. It's amazing to think we have dealt with this challenge and accomplished so much without ever being in a room together.

Somehow it was enough that Jamie and I were in our cockpit together trying to fly and land this huge Dreamliner, wherever and whenever that may be.

Two imperfect people joined together to form a strong (but not perfect) ParentPreneur team.

We have each other, our kids, and Zoomie. We can do this.

And we feel that we are stronger as a company and as a team than we were BEFORE the pandemic.

WE SAY: When leading a big team, realize you are never going to make everyone happy, so make the best decisions for the whole and stick with them.

Between our CertifiKID/Macaroni KID HQ team and the Macaroni KID publisher community, we had never been in this position before where our decisions were impacting so many people's lives and livelihoods. We quickly learned that, as hard as we tried, we would never please everyone or get unanimous support for any decision, and there would be unhappy people.

You should listen and understand the concerns, but it is your job as the leader to make the best decisions for the entire business and community you serve, explain those decisions, and then move on—and to do so consistently, not occasionally. Of course, if you make a mistake, own up to it and make a change, but then move on again.

Your job is not to appease people. It is to lead them to where you are trying to go and to earn their trust and respect. If you invest the time, solicit and absorb the feedback, do the research, and consider all your options, you should be confident in the path you choose and not look back. But if you do, those you are leading will be right behind you every step of the way.

· 13 ·

That's a Wrap

SHE SAID: I loved writing this book. It was cathartic.

Has this book inspired you to want to jump into starting a business? How about jumping into business with the person next to you in bed? Or are you thinking, those poor people need a glass of wine and to chill for a bit?

There are many times I find myself daydreaming about the life I would be living if I had never mentioned my idea to Brian in our messy minivan twelve years ago. I imagine all the incredible birthday parties I would have thrown for my kids, the different friend groups and social connections I would have had, the getaways where I would have easily unplugged, the soccer teams I would have coached, and the activities I would have gotten my kids into. I am sure I would have been "that mom" that made everything special. I feel a tinge of sadness as I mourn the life that my kids might have lived and all I have sacrificed as well.

However, I know if I had not started this business, I would have always felt like something was missing in my life. I am sure I would have eventually started something, or maybe my blog would have taken off, or I would have joined one of those social selling networks, or better yet, become a Macaroni KID publisher.

I believe everything does happen for a reason and this business was my calling. It has been beyond challenging and required drive and persistence, but the fact that I have found a business that can keep me motivated and excited even twelve years later is exactly what I need. I wake up every morning eager for what the day will bring because I know there will be something new!

There is also the impact this business has had on our marriage, which is significant. It was not what we signed up for together when we said "I do" over seventeen years ago. It's not like you can switch costumes on the weekend and say today we are just "spouses Jamie and Brian" or "Mom and Dad" and then on Monday at 8:00 a.m. we are "CEO Jamie and President Brian."

Come 11:00 p.m., I may be drooling on my pillow trying to talk to Brian about the vendor contract issue we are dealing with as his eyes glaze over, and then dealing with his grouchiness the next morning when I am on his case about writing this book instead of giving him ten minutes to get his Starbucks. Outside of mom guilt, I have also had spouse guilt over all the time Brian has lost as well from this incredibly busy life we live.

I know for sure I could never have started or run this business without Brian, and especially not taken it to the level of success we have achieved. He is everything I am not. He brings the professionalism, perfectionism, polish, and reasoning that I completely lack (and he is way nicer than I am!). We are opposite in so many ways that we complement each other, which is a homerun when it comes to business and probably very hard to deal with unless you are married! Oh, and he is my editor like he was for this book!

Though, here's a secret: I curse a lot in this book, and Brian doesn't at all. We're the opposite in real life. This shows how different you can be behind a screen versus in person!

Despite all the ups and downs, if you and your spouse or partner have that itch, I urge you to go for it. The benefits of building a business together outnumber any of the challenges. Our time is spent in one silo, not separate ones, which is a beautiful place to be.

Plus, to have your kids watch your every move and truly learn how to run and operate a business is priceless. You will be talking business in front of them as you give them baths, drive them to soccer games, and everywhere in between—and it will be hard! And they will also see you work together as a unit, multitask, triage, create, show respect and compassion, fight and make up, and share the joys of success and disappointments of setbacks. In addition to the nuts and bolts of running a business, just think of the benefits of this real-world education on their growth and development.

Sometimes when we are at a restaurant and we see an old couple sitting there with absolutely nothing to say to one another, it hits me. I realize there is no chance that will ever be us. We have enough from the past decade to keep us laughing for the next ten decades to come. It has been such a ride and there is no one else I would want to be next to in that minivan.

HE SAID: I hated writing this book. It was torture.

We finally got the kids off to camp, which was a monumental undertaking. It was our first weekend alone together, and we could finally relax after the whirlwind of the *Shark Tank* airing, *The View* appearance, and the O'Leary Summit. Jamie's focus was almost entirely on this book. Like *Shark Tank*, I fought it.

> ME: Do we have to jump into something so quickly? We did the *Shark Tank* application last summer. Can't we take a breath this summer?
>
> JAMIE: Now's the time. If we wait, our moment will pass. It won't be that much work. I'll do most of it.
>
> ME: It will be A LOT of work. For both of us. Timing isn't great for me at the firm, as you know.
>
> JAMIE: I need this. I am really excited just thinking about it and have a lot of ideas. I have read a hundred books in the last few weeks and know exactly what we need to do, who our audience is, and why they will love it.
>
> ME: Fine. But you must promise me something. You cannot get frustrated every time I'm not keeping up with you. I will do what I need to do, like always, but I beg you to not lose patience with me during the process. Okay?
>
> JAMIE: DEAL.

Just as I was grimacing and feeling stressed about how behind I was on my chapter contributions, I came across this from former President Jimmy and Rosalynn Carter on the occasion of their seventy-fifth wedding anniversary:

> Jimmy and Rosalyn Carter have been happily married since 1946. "The best thing I ever did was marrying Rosalynn. . . . That's a pinnacle in my life."[1]
>
> That's not to say it's been easy sailing all through. Take the time the couple decided to write a book together. "It's the worst problem we've ever had since we've been married."
>
> "That was a terrible experience," Rosalynn agreed.[2]
>
> Alternating chapters, Mr. Carter told Piers Morgan about the resistance he received when editing his wife's writing: "It would be like God had given her this text at Mt. Sinai and she had brought it down and presented it to me in stone."[3]

This made me feel better.

Of course, Jamie didn't keep her promise—that is, she got frustrated and impatient with me A LOT during the book-writing process. I couldn't keep up with her as usual. But we did finish the book like I promised her we would, though after the pandemic and acquisition! I'm fully gray now with a *bigger* bald spot and my kids think I've aged five years. But, like always, she was right to push. Our story is compelling, and we have something meaningful to say. I hope you agree.

Despite my struggles, this book and the process of writing it has also helped me appreciate Jamie in new ways. I cannot describe the amount of pride I have in her—what she does for me and our family, what she does for our business and team, and what she has accomplished against the odds. She has always been underestimated and proven the naysayers wrong every time. She's the last woman standing.

Early on, after we launched the business, someone who was working with us said to me they thought Jamie was a "shark." This was a compliment. The point was, she was fearless and relentless. While she carried internally this fear that the business could end tomorrow (and still does!), she never showed it externally. She only showed resolve, confidence, and perseverance.

I've never met anyone who works harder or moves faster, which is saying a lot because I work with some exceptional people. She is not a traditional leader, though I think this is her secret sauce. She leads by example and based on her knowledge, experience, and instinct. She helps others succeed by showing them how as opposed to telling them how.

And she has brought the most exciting dynamic into our lives. The people we have met and places we have been have enriched us in countless ways. She thinks of the old couple at the restaurant, but I think of the old couple that walks around our neighborhood block every day. I notice how they, too, never say a word to each other. When Jamie and I walk around the block, we are always talking, brainstorming, reminiscing, and usually laughing hysterically. It's an intellectually active relationship. It didn't have to be this way, but I am grateful that it is.

I always thought I had a good business acumen but when I headed down the law lane, I never expected to test that theory and birdie in my head. Jamie brought this ParentPreneur opportunity into my life when I wasn't expecting it. I've taken her lead, leaned into it, and I've loved it—okay, not every minute of it, because it has been a tough balancing act for me, but most of it. And I've gained skills and experiences I never would have otherwise that I use every day in my dual roles for the benefit of our business and team, and my firm and clients. I have Jamie to thank for this.

Most importantly, working with Jamie has been the greatest gift for me and for us.

WE SAY: If we survived *Shark Tank*, a pandemic, an acquisition, and writing this book, we can survive anything (and so can you).

We are just your average parents, when it all comes down to it. We dealt with diapers and tantrums, and now we deal with middle school drama. We are far from perfect in all aspects of our lives. We have no formal training or educational background in business. We just somehow make it all work. We believe part of it is doing it all together. We know this won't work for every marriage or partnership, but we are proof it can. We hope you will take the plunge!

And it doesn't need to be a business venture, though we do think there are more emerging ParentPreneurs than ever before and hope this book is a catalyst for that trend. Find something to work on with your spouse or partner that is not about your kids or your respective day jobs. Maybe it's joining a committee or association. Maybe it's doing something charitable. Maybe it's being co-team manager or coach on your kid's soccer team. Maybe it's doing freelance writing. Get creative. Make the time. And do it TOGETHER.

The world has changed, and we are never going back. Remote and flexible work is the present and the future. There is no longer the excuse or the inevitable reality that you and your spouse or partner will be ships passing in the night, at different workplaces, or one at home and one in the office. Ignore the old stereotypes and traditional barriers.

There are more opportunities than ever before to be in the same place—home—for at least some of your work life! So why not make "work-life balance" apply to you AND your spouse or partner, and not just YOU. It won't be a picnic or without its sacrifices. But we are proof that mixing marriage and business, and being ParentPreneurs together, can be bonding and enriching in unimaginable ways.

Notes

1. "Jimmy and Rosalynn Carter through the Years," CNN Politics, August 20, 2015, https://www.cnn.com/2015/08/20/politics/gallery/jimmy-carter-ro salynn-carter/index.html.

2. Caitlin McDevitt, "Carters: Writing a Book Together was Terrible," citing Jimmy and Rosalynn Carter interview with CNN's Piers Morgan, *Politico*, https://www.politico.com/blogs/click/2012/01/carters-writing-a-book -together-was-terrible-111358.

3. Saeed Ahmed, "Jimmy and Rosalynn Carter Just Became the Longest-Married Presidential Couple," CNN Politics, October 18, 2019, https:// www.cnn.com/2019/10/18/politics/jimmy-rosalynn-carter-longest-married -presidential-couple-trnd/index.html.

Acknowledgments

It takes a village of people in your corner to succeed as a ParentPreneur. We have been fortunate to have this kind of support both personally and in business from many people over the years. There are too many to mention by name, but we feel several are worth noting and thanking.

First, our amazing children Noah and Lila, to whom we dedicate this book. They have been active participants in our business since day one and have never made us feel guilty for it. To be a ParentPreneur, you must have kids who will let you be one. We are grateful that ours have.

Our parents, Gary, Sandy, and Carol, and our late dad, Jimmy. For all the love, support, and encouragement so that we could dream big and realize those dreams. And for their willingness to drop anything or do anything (in Gary's case, working tirelessly for free for eleven years) to help us get to where we were trying to go.

Our siblings, Mindy, Erik, and Lisa. For being great sounding boards and contributors at every stage on our journey.

Our *ParentPreneurs* team, who encouraged us to write this book, believed that people would be interested in what we have to say, and then helped us to make it all happen: Rachel, Liza, and the Liza Dawson Associates team; Suzanne, Elaine, and the Rowman & Littlefield team; Rea; and our in-house editor extraordinaire, Kim.

Our CertifiKID team, the best and most supportive team anyone could ever ask for: Gary, Leslie, Amie, Bien, Kim, Randi, Olga, Beth, Barbara, Rachel H., Amy F., Kelly, Cynthia, David, An, Lara, Jennifer, Stephanie, Joan, Kristina, Miranda, Rachel R., and others who have worked for us and made invaluable contributions to our business and story.

Our Macaroni KID team and publisher community, which took a leap of faith on us and inspire us every day: Kayt, Charlotte, Kat, Lindsay, Noelle, Zulema, Kara, Julie, Anu, Laura, and countless others who have worked for us, supported us, and made important contributions since our acquisition. And Joyce and Eric, for calling us back and handing us the baton.

Kevin O'Leary (aka "Mr. Wonderful"), who saw something in us in the Tank that day and decided we were people he wanted to be in business with, as opposed to kicking us out. And for his generous foreword!

The O'Leary team, which has supported and guided us so well since 2019: Alex, Nancy, Matthew, and Dom; and the O'Leary Shark Tank companies which are a great resource and support system.

Shark Tank, for admitting us to the Harvard of entrepreneur reality shows, and our producers Jeremy and Alan for believing in us.

Our stellar team of external advisors and consultants who always treated us like more than a mom-and-pop shop, even when we were one: Doug, Michelle, Kelly, John, Brian G., Franklin, and the Nelson Mullins team; Brent, Michael, Deidre, and the Hausfeld team; Bill, Kristin, Zack, and the Baker Tilly team; Liz and the Huntington team; Avanee and the Citibank team; Dorene and the Beecher Carlson team; Mike and the RBC team; Jeanne and the RPA team; Jackie and the NFP team; Frank; Andrew; Brian S.; Lisa; Dottie; and Stephanie.

Tom Heath. If you read the book, you'll know why.

All the businesses that took a chance on us, partnered with us, and helped us get to where we are today.

All our loyal subscribers and followers who have stuck with us and whom we do our best to serve every day.

And our "family and friends" network who have rooted us on and helped spread the word every step of the way.

Thank you all from the bottom of our hearts.

Index

159

About the Authors

Jamie Ratner is the CEO and cofounder of CertifiKID, a recognized "best deal" website for parents. Over the past decade and with CertifiKID's recent acquisition of Macaroni KID, Jamie has grown CertifiKID from a regional deal website to one of the largest parent-focused digital media and advertising companies in the country, reaching millions of families nationwide and backed by an investment from *Shark Tank*'s Kevin O'Leary (aka "Mr. Wonderful"). Jamie was named one of the region's "Brightest Young Business Leaders" by the *Washington Business Journal* and one of Greater Washington's top women business leaders by Washington SmartCEO. So, Jamie knows a thing or two about what parents want. A soccer mom and entrepreneur (aka "Mompreneur"), she's one of the country's leading experts in the daily deal, parent, and digital media space.

Brian Ratner is the cofounder and president of CertifiKID. He is also a founding partner of Hausfeld, a global litigation law firm headquartered in Washington, DC, where he serves as Global Co-Chair of the firm and specializes in global antitrust and commercial litigation on behalf of businesses of all sizes and across industries. Brian has been featured on the Washington, DC, *Super Lawyers* list since 2014; "The Legal 500 2020 Hall of Fame" and "Leading Lawyers" lists since 2014; the *Who's Who Legal* "Global Leader," "Thought Leader," and "Recommended Lawyer for Competition/Plaintiff" lists since 2018; and the *Lawdragon* "500 Leading Lawyers in America" list for the past three years.

Jamie and Brian Ratner live in Potomac, Maryland, with their two children. And more personally,

> Jamie is cheap. Brian is a big tipper.
> Jamie cooks. Brian cleans.
> Jamie makes messes. Brian mops them up.
> Jamie writes. Brian edits.
> Jamie creates and conceives. Brian implements and executes.
> Jamie is a doer. Brian is a talker.
> Jamie is the first to arrive. Brian is the last to leave.
> Jamie doesn't care what people think, but she sometimes should. Brian does care, but he sometimes shouldn't.
> Jamie is like lightning—fast and efficient. Brian is like a storm— slow-moving and methodical.
> Jamie is a glass half empty kind of gal. Brian is a glass half full kind of guy.

Together, they make the perfect combination to throw a party, run a business, manage a community of hundreds of moms (and some dads) across the country in big cities and small towns, or even make a good impression on *Shark Tank*.

Together, they are *ParentPreneurs*.

To learn more about CertifiKID and Macaroni KID, visit www.certifi kid.com and www.macaronikid.com.